I Wrote
This Book
on Purpose...

(So You Can Know Yours)
2nd edition

John W. Stanko

urbanpress

I Wrote This Book on Purpose...So You Can Know Yours, 2nd Edition
by John W. Stanko
Copyright © 1998, 2019 John W. Stanko

ISBN # 978-1-63360-104-8

For Worldwide Distribution Printed in the U.S.A.

Urban Press
P.O. Box 8881
Pittsburgh, PA 15221-0881 USA
412.646.2780
www.urbanpress.us

Endorsement

"This is an immenseley important book that will help you think about who you are—and who you're not. In my writing and consulting, the issue of purpose comes up time and time again. Not only am I now more equipped to help others on their own purpose journey, but John has helped me embrace my own. I'm putting his ideas into practice in my own personal and professional life. Time spent reading *I Wrote This Book on Purpose* will pay dividends in your life for years to come."

—Patrick Lencioni, president of *The Table Group* and best-selling author

Table of Contents

INTRODUCTION

"To have a great purpose to work for, a purpose larger than ourselves, is one of the secrets of making life significant, for then the meaning and worth of the individual overflow his personal borders and survive his death." —Will Durant

It all began in November 1991. I was visiting a Nazarene church in Pismo Beach, California, and for the first time, I was scheduled to teach my seminar entitled, "Effectiveness: Functioning in Your Purpose." The context was a "Come and Worship!" event sponsored by Worship International, the ministry division of Integrity Music.

I was apprehensive, to say the least, as I waited for the session to begin. I rehearsed again in my mind all the objections I had raised when Steve, the director, suggested we offer the class on an experimental basis. "These people are musicians and song leaders," I told Steve, "and they won't be interested in what I have to say. They want technical and musical help and aren't looking for a philosophical discussion on life purpose." Steve firmly insisted that we proceed, however, so I stood at the podium waiting to see if anyone would come, pessimistically convinced they would not.

To my surprise and relief, people did come. To my greater surprise and relief, so did the Lord. I sensed His favor as I taught the principles of purpose that had become so pertinent in my life. As I taught, I noticed some were deeply moved and even wept during parts of my presentation. The 75 minutes went quickly and people gathered around to ask questions and express appreciation after the session was over. Steve was right: If I taught it, they would come.

People continued to come to that class for the next five years as I offered it at every "Come and Worship!" weekend. My purpose class was consistently one of the most popular classes on our seminar evaluations. When we went "international," I had the chance to present the class in Malaysia, Singapore, Hong Kong, Taiwan, England, Australia, and many other countries.

The results were always the same: People were deeply touched and affected. I have many testimonies from people who made radical life-direction changes because of what they heard in my class. Later, I expanded the session into an all-day seminar and thousands have come to learn how to identify and engage their life's purpose. That all-day seminar formed the basis for part of this book.

When I first began my journey into purpose— both personal application and teaching others—there was not much written material pertaining to the topic of purpose. That's why I wrote my first book to meet the demand for more purpose material people could study after my seminar. That book, *Life is a Gold Mine: Can*

You Dig It? has sold thousands of copies, is published and distributed in several African nations, and was translated for distribution in China, India, and other countries. In 2017, I published a twentieth-anniversary edition, and have supplemented it with a *Life is a Gold Mine Daily Devotional.*

When I first authored *I Wrote This Book on Purpose* in 1998, I included an audio cassette with the book. That tells you a bit about how much the world has changed since then. Not only has the world changed, however, but I have changed as well. Since 1998, I have written or re-written 38 books, including *Unlocking the Power of Your Purpose, The Price of Leadership, Beyond Purpose*, and six daily devotionals, all of which contain material on life purpose. I also started two companies, PurposeQuest Inc. and PurposeQuest International, along with a website, www.purposequest.com, to house all my material on purpose. It is accurate to say that the creation of material to help others find their purpose became a full-time pursuit for me. Now it's time to revise this book, and I have collected plenty of material in the last twenty-five years, and that will make this book twice the length of the original work.

I've never had anyone challenge me on the validity, worth, or biblical correctness of my purpose presentation. Almost everyone intuitively knows the truth about purpose. Most people familiar with the Bible have at one time or another quoted to someone the words of Romans 8:28: "All things work together for good for those who love God and are called according to His *purpose*" (emphasis added). Perhaps they even know Proverbs 16:4, "The LORD HAS MADE EVERYTHING FOR ITS OWN *purpose*, even the wicked for the day of evil" (NASB, emphasis added).

Many have found that talking about purpose, however, is a lot easier than defining it for themselves in a personal way. I wrote this book on purpose to help you get beyond *agreeing* that you have a purpose to the point where you can *clearly state the reason* you were born. I'm more convinced than ever before that it's possible for everyone to do that, even you.

In my travels and research, I've met many wonderful people who have the same burden I do: to see people doing not just good things, but the best things they were created to do. I've also found that other groups, with differing philosophical perspectives, have pursued this topic and have produced some interesting books and articles before I ever started my quest for purpose. For instance, Laurence G. Boldt wrote these words in his book, *How to Find the Work You Love*:

> The quest for the work you love—it all begins with the two simple questions: Who am I? And What in the world am I doing here? While as old as humanity itself, these perennial questions are born anew in every man and woman who is privileged to walk upon this earth. Every sane man and woman, at some point in his or her life, is confronted by these questions—some while but children; more in adolescence and youth; still more at midlife or

when facing retirement; and even the toughest customers at the death of a loved one or when they themselves have a brush with death. Yes, somewhere, sometime, we all find ourselves face to face with the questions, Who am I? and What am I here for?

And we do make some attempt to answer them. We ask our parents and teachers, and it seems they do not know. They refer us to political and religious institutions, which often crank out canned answers devoid of personal meaning. Some even tell us that life has no meaning, save for eating and breeding. Most of us are smart enough to recognize that canned answers or begging the question will not do. We must find real answers for ourselves. But that takes more heart and effort than we are often willing to give.[1]

I agree with much of what Mr. Boldt wrote. I can confirm from my experience that almost everyone faces the issue of purpose at one time or another. You are facing it, or you wouldn't be reading this book or trying to answer the questions: Who am I? and What am I here for? People begin their quest for answers at different stages of life, some in childhood and some at retirement.

Furthermore, religious institutions sometimes offer "canned answers" that leave people with simplistic solutions to their purpose questions: How can I know God's will for my life? How then can I do it? Often people tell me that they are here "to do the will of God," "to glorify God," "to serve others," or "to worship Him." The problem is that these answers fall short, for you must go further to find the *specific* will of God for your life, *what it is* that will glorify God, *how* you can serve others, and *what it means* to worship God beyond singing a hymn or chorus on Sunday morning.

Since the first edition of this book hit the market, I witnessed the release of the best-selling book in the history of publishing (next to the Bible): Rick Warren's *The Purpose Driven Life*. Despite Pastor Warren's impact, I still find that people are searching and digging for purpose more frantically than ever. In a sense, as purpose possibilities have expanded exponentially, it has created another purpose question in peoples' minds: *With so many options for what I can do, how do I know what I should do?*

The pursuit of answers "takes more heart and effort than we are often willing to give," as Mr. Boldt wrote. It's so much easier to settle for pat answers or to have someone else define who we are, but that's like putting a band-aid on a major laceration. It may look good and even cover the wound, but it won't necessarily bring the desired long-term results, clarity, or fulfillment.

I take issue with Mr. Boldt, however, as to the source of the insight and revelation necessary to answer the questions raised. Mr. Boldt also wrote a book entitled *Zen and the Art of Making a Living*; the answer for him can come from many sources, since Zen promotes the total enlightenment of an individual through meditation and work. The answer for my questions doesn't come from self-enlightenment or a guru; my answers come from the One who created me and assigned me a purpose according to His will.

It isn't uncommon for those who discuss the topic of purpose at some point to refer to purpose as a life's calling or vocation. The word *vocation* comes from the Latin word *vocare*, which means *to call*. Originally, a person could be called or have the vocation of a shoe maker or a butcher. (Eventually a vocation or call became associated with a religious calling to the priesthood or some other form of ministry.) However broadly or narrowly you define calling, the concept assumes there is some intelligent being or entity doing the calling. I cannot conceive of how an activity can be the one calling out to a person.

When I seek to serve God and cooperate with His plan, I have found my life to have meaning and direction. As the psalmist wrote, "My help comes from the Lord, the maker of heaven and earth" (Psalm 121:2). The designer of a thing is the perfect one to define the purpose of the designed, and that is why I look to, even expect, the God of heaven and earth to answer my purpose questions. Mr. Boldt also wrote:

> Finding the work you love is not a cerebral process. It is not a matter of figuring something out through a process of rational analysis. It is a process of opening yourself and beginning to pay attention to what you respond to with energy and enthusiasm. Pay attention to the people, events, and activities in

the outside world that evoke the strongest response from you. Pay attention as well to your inside world, to the inspirations and intuitions that most excite you. From within and without, let yourself be moved. Listen to your own heart and learn to trust what it is saying.[2]

My desire is to help you listen and be moved to see yourself not as others see you, but as God sees you. With that in mind, this book is a combination workbook and inspirational reader. I want you to be inspired and directed as I share with you a collection of quotes, personal testimonies, and real-life stories I've collected over the last twenty-plus years. I also want you to be equipped with greater understanding of the whole topic of purpose, so I have included some further insights not found in that original tape or my first edition. To replace that cassette tape, I have more than doubled the size of *I Wrote This Book on Purpose* from the original version.

I did that by including the material from a program I once had called *PurposeCoach*, an online program that looked at purpose from four different perspectives: ministry, the marketplace, the church, and the individual. The format of this book will include a chapter from a seminar I taught called *Getting Your Life Back on Track: A Study of Purpose and Goals* (that was the original material in *I Wrote This Book on Purpose*). Those seven chapters have a word in the title that begins with the letter P, and summarize a biblical overview of material to help you identify your purpose. Following each seminar chapter will be a chapter from my *PurposeCoach* lessons, and those will include case studies and teaching from the four perspectives of one's life.

Then I am including an entire section of what I call a PurposeChallenge. Since 2001, I have written a weekly online entry called *The Monday Memo.* As I update this book, I have written 880 *Monday Memos.* In 2010, I directed people to my website where I had included a brief PurposeQuest survey that enabled me to give those who took it some feedback on where I thought they were in their PurposeQuest. After they took the survey, I wrote a number of follow up *Memos* that led to them taking the survey again in four months. I am including that Challenge in its entirety for you to do the same. As you will learn when we get to that section, purpose does not stand alone, but goes hand-in-hand with goal-setting, time management, values, and other important life disciplines.

I hope you will write down your thoughts or impressions as you read. Jot down ideas and concepts you want to research or study later. As you set your mind and heart to seek your purpose, it's important to pay attention to your thoughts and impressions calling out to you—as you will learn in the PurposeChallenge section. Those thoughts may not make sense when you hear or think of them, but it's important that you "honor" them as they come.

Malcolm Gladwell in his book *Outliers* expressed the belief that a person will be an expert or top performer in his or her field when they have devoted 10,000 hours of concentrated study or effort in that area or discipline.

Author Seth Godin urges his readers to find something they do well, perfect it to become one of the best in the world, and then give the rest of their lives to expressing that one thing.

This book will not debate whether the premises of these two men are true. I decided to take both men at their word, and I have invested more than 10,000 hours in one thing—helping others find purpose—because I wanted to be one of the best, most skilled, and anointed purpose coaches in the world. I will leave the results and the "standings" of where I rank in God's hands, but I have paid the price and focused my attention to be the best I can be.

The last thirty years have been the most fulfilling of my life as I have traveled to 40 countries to address audiences large and small about purpose. Along the way, I have had one-on-one purpose sessions with thousands of people. I have concentrated on my own purpose and saw my understanding of it change ever so slightly, but the change released an avalanche of creativity in me that has yet to cease. I've seen many come to a better understanding of who they are and why they're here, and my work has been fulfilling and rewarding.

Despite the explosion of purpose material, coaches, seminars, books, and purpose-theme movies, people are still asking the questions mentioned earlier. They want to know their purpose. This indicates that much work remains to be done for us to be a purpose-driven people. *I Wrote This Book on Purpose* to further the quest of every person to find the reason they were born. I now present the second edition to continue my life's work to help you be a person of purpose. With that in mind, let's get to work.

John W. Stanko
Pittsburgh PA
January 2019

CHAPTER 1
Productivity is a Priority

*"This is the true joy in life, the being used for
a purpose recognized by yourself as a mighty
one; the being thoroughly worn out before you
are thrown on the scrap heap; the being a force
of Nature instead of a feverish selfish little clod
of ailments and grievances complaining that
the world will not devote itself to making you
happy."* – George Bernard Shaw

Jim was sitting in my office after having heard me speak on purpose in a church setting. The message worked on and in him, as it tends to do after someone hears it, and eventually Jim set an appointment to come and talk about his life purpose. He was a successful but unfulfilled professional who sensed there was more for him to do and be than what he was currently doing. I started our session with my usual questions: What would you do if you had all the money you needed to live on? What gives you joy? What comes naturally and easily for you to do?

Without hesitation, Jim proceeded to answer my questions, which was a bit unusual, for usually I had to work to "prime the pump" for those who came to see me because many are not comfortable talking about themselves and who they are. It was not what Jim said, however, that caught my attention; it was how he said it.

As he began to tell me how much he loved the outdoors—hiking, fishing, canoeing, and the like—he had a look on his face like he was enduring a root canal. He swung his head from side to side with a grimace on his face as he reported his passion for all things outdoors. After a few minutes, I asked him what I thought was an obvious question: Why do you look like you are having open heart surgery without any anesthetic?

Jim was stunned when I asked him that. He paused to think and then responded, "I guess it's because I don't see how I can possibly do those things more than I am now. I have a family to support and responsibilities." After that, he sat in silence as he continued to assess the impact and repercussions of my question.

My advice to Jim was to stop trying to figure out *how* he was going to fulfill his purpose, but rather to focus on *what* his purpose was. After all, God wanted him to fulfill his purpose more than he did, and would help him if he accepted and then rested in the reality of who he was, who God had made him to be.

Jim left my office and never looked back. Today, he is the founder of the nonprofit organization, Outdoor Immersion, an organization dedicated "to share the beauty, peace and transforming power of creation with those who need it." He works with the Wounded Warriors program and escorts youth on outdoor adventures geared to help them find another part of life beyond the city life they know so well. Since he accepted his purpose, many people have donated the equipment he needs to help others embrace the great outdoors. It is always a joy to see Jim post on social media what he is doing, and I always go back to that remarkable session we had when he looked like he was in agony. Recently, he wrote me to say that he was heading to speak to a group about what he does, telling me how energized and grateful he is to be a man of purpose.

That's the power of purpose. It directs your life and allows you to find the fulfillment and productivity you have always wanted. Don't think for one minute that God isn't interested in productivity—He is. When God first created Adam and Eve, He gave them some instructions: "God blessed them and said to them, 'Be fruitful and increase in number; fill the earth and subdue it'" (Genesis 1:28). It later says that "the Lord took the man and put him in the Garden of Eden to work it and take care of it" (Genesis 2:15). That tells us that God didn't create Adam and Eve and consequently all of mankind to muddle through life here on earth. He put us here to do something specific that is uniquely suited for each one of us according to our skills, gifts, interests, and life experience.

Peter, one of Jesus' original disciples and apostles, wrote an interesting passage in his second epistle. Peter is an interesting study in purpose. He was a fisherman who was working in his family business when Jesus met him. Jesus predicted that he would be a "fisher of men," defining Peter's area of productivity—he would lead people to know the truth about Jesus. From that time on, this simple businessman took on new meaning and purpose.

Eventually, he became the spokesman and leader for a movement that would spread throughout the Roman Empire. Today, we still study his words and life. He was neither a scholar nor a religious leader. He was a man who found his purpose and here we are, 2,000 years later, quoting from a letter that this man wrote. That's the power of purpose. I highlight what he wrote in my *Getting Your Life Back on Track* seminar:

> For this very reason, make every effort to add to your faith goodness; and to goodness, knowledge; and to knowledge, self-control; and to self-control, perseverance and to perseverance, godliness; and to godliness, brotherly kindness, and to brotherly kindness, love. For if you possess these qualities in increasing measure, they will keep you from being *ineffective* or *unproductive* in your knowledge of our Lord Jesus Christ (2 Peter 1:5-8, emphasis added).

Notice the emphasis on holiness *and* right behavior in those verses. In most cases, the church has focused its attention over the years on holiness but seldom on the practical expressions of that holiness—apart from the rules of "don't do this or that." Peter emphasized more than holiness, writing that we should increase in our holiness or else we may be found *ineffective* and *unproductive*. Let's take a closer look at those two words as they appear in the original Greek that Peter used when he wrote.

The word *ineffective* comes from the Greek word *argos* and is translated "barren" in the more traditional King James Version. Research shows that its other meanings included "lazy" and "shunning the labor that one ought to perform." Each of us is assigned a labor or life work that is related to our purpose. Finding our purpose frees us to fulfill our labor and causes us—even drives us—to do things on purpose. What's more, focused labor is not just busy work. Focused labor leads to productivity, fruit that will remain, because it is what we are best-suited and skilled to do.

There are many people, especially believing Christians, who are content with doctrinal correctness, but don't see the need for personal productivity. They believe that as long as they *don't* do certain things, like rob banks or watch bad movies, and as long as they go to church regularly, and as long as they believe the right doctrine about the Holy Spirit or spiritual gifts or the end times, then they are doing God's will. They are content to watch others function in their purpose and live vicariously off other people's success instead of amassing their own collection of testimonies.

It would be easy to label these Christians as lazy and perhaps they are. M. Scott Peck, the late Christian author and psychiatrist, maintained that all laziness is rooted in fear, and I agree with him. The lack of productivity among believers is because we are afraid—fearful of getting ahead of the Lord, of missing the Lord, of criticism, of drawing attention to ourselves, and the list goes on and on. We are waiting on the Lord to drop something out of the sky that won't require us to work beyond our self-imposed, 40-hour weekly allotment. I've known some who have retreated into their families, using the excuse that they can't be productive until their children grow up, their finances improve, or until the system (whether it be political, economic, or educational) allows them greater access to power or opportunity.

Then there are non-Christians who find all kinds of life philosophies promising to produce peace and harmony. These are legitimate goals, but what good are they as an end unto themselves? Have those who discovered peace and harmony founded schools or hospitals? Have they produced movements alleviating any world problems? Too often they are selfish, self-centered exercises, giving lip service to serving mankind, but in reality focusing only or primarily on the needs of the individual. Buddhism, which has influenced many people and movements, has as its stated goal enlightenment, which is freedom from suffering. Christianity's stated goal is that we identify with Christ in His sufferings as we follow Him and serve mankind in our assigned purpose.

Every Christian who puts his or her faith in the resurrection of Christ should do exceptional things in this lifetime. After all, if God can raise the dead, He can do anything. Unfortunately, some are content to believe the right thing without ever applying the power of that belief to everyday life. Many are also content to lead purposeless lives, feeling that this somehow glorifies the God of creation because they did not make any mistakes. They did not do much, but they did not fail. This too is selfishness and doesn't lead to any distinction between a Christian and a non-Christian.

Finally, there are some who are happy just to keep busy, without asking whether their busy-ness is leading to any productive outcome. Charles Handy wrote in *The Age of Unreason,*

> It is not the devil who finds work for idle hands to do, it is our own human instincts which make us want to contribute to our world, to be useful, and to matter in some way to other people; to have a reason to get up in the morning.[3]

To ignore this instinct to make a difference is to ignore one of the basic drives God has given us all, a desire to define who we are and what God expects us to do—and then do it.

The Centers for Disease Control and Prevention report that more people die at 9:00 on Monday morning than at any other time of day and on any other day of the week. Why? Perhaps these busy or retired people find no meaning in their lives. They've divorced their existence from any meaningful philosophy of life that allows them to feel like they're making a difference so they check out. Perhaps they just can't face another meaningless week of drudgery and death is their only escape.

The loss from unproductive lives isn't just in people dying (and some are "dead" even when they're alive) before their time. There are greater losses than this according to Laurence Boldt:

> Failing to find the work you love has costs, not only to your self-esteem, relationships, health, and creativity, but to your world. As a human community, we all lose when people's creative abilities do not find expression in constructive, purposeful action. We lose in terms of needless human suffering and untapped human potential. Around the globe, useless, even degrading work steals the spirit and saps the joy from the lives of millions, while much necessary work goes undone. Giving your gifts benefits the world, not only through the direct contributions you make and the joy you radiate, but through the living example you provide others of what is possible for them. *Determine to lay your part in creating the kind of world you want to live in.*[4]

Now, let's get back to Peter's second word that I referred to earlier. The word *unproductive* is the Greek word *akarpos* and is rendered *unfruitful* in the King James Version. It literally means "not yielding the fruit that one ought to yield." The fruit that we are to bear is more than internal; it's also external. It's more than being a nice person. Your "niceness" or kindness should translate into effective labor. It should relate to work that's connected to your purpose in life. Jesus said, "You did not choose me, but I chose you and appointed you to go and bear fruit, fruit that will remain" (John 15:16). Now let's look at some historical examples of people who produced what I call fruit:

- In his lifetime, Charles Wesley wrote almost 9,000 hymns.

- Charles' brother, John Wesley, preached 40,000 sermons in his lifetime and traveled 250,000 miles on horseback, the equivalent of ten circuits of the globe along the equator.

- Charles Haddon Spurgeon, the great British 19th-century preacher, preached to 10 million people in his lifetime.

Let's look outside the realm of church or missions work:

- Cyrus McCormick, 19th-century inventor and business innovator, not only invented the reaper, but also created such modern business techniques as the written money-back guarantee, a guaranteed sale price to buyers, interest-free financing to farmers who desperately needed the equipment, and service and repairs for the machines he sold.

- George Washington Carver, African-American 19th-century scientist, discovered more than 300 uses for the peanut and more than 100 uses for the sweet potato, thus providing much-needed markets for crops unique to the southern area of the United States.

- James Michener, American novelist, found an entertaining way to combine history and story-telling. I learned more history from his novels than from almost any other source. Although his books were long, I could not put them down once I began. His books are still strong sellers even after his death.

How productive are you? What are you doing on purpose? Is your increasing knowledge of God leading to effectiveness and productivity? Or are you content to sit back smugly satisfied that having a life philosophy and correct beliefs are all that are required of you? In chapter three, I want to encourage you to get more specific about your purpose, for without that you cannot hope to fulfill God's desire (or your own) for your productivity and meaning. Before you go on, reflect on these questions at the end of this chapter. Write down where your thoughts lead you. Then move on to your PurposeCoach lesson in chapter two before we return to our purpose discussion in chapter three.

What is your greatest area of **productivity**? Is it cooking? I had one woman tell me that she sensed "the presence of God" every time she opened her oven door and felt the heat caress her face. Is it baking? I talked with a woman in Montana who was known as the "cookie lady." People told me that she "constantly" made cookies, put a few of them in plastic bags, included a piece of paper with a Bible verse on it, and went through her small town distributing them to those she met.

What is your greatest area of **effectiveness**? Is it people in need? Or children? A past issue of *Southern Living* magazine talked about a man name Doyle Cagle, who some would say is "just" a school bus driver. But this bus driver gave children who made the honor roll $3 out of his own pocket. If a child forgot his backpack, Mr. Cagle went back to get it and delivered it to the child at school. He belongs to the PTA for all three schools to which he delivers children. One parent said, "Every child thinks Mr. Cagle likes him best. He is what God wants us to be." Who and what does God want you to be?

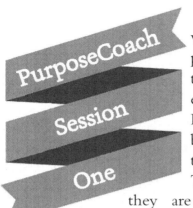

As I stated in the previous chapter, I have had few people challenge me about the truth that God created everyone with a purpose. People have no problem believing and even seeing that others have purpose. The problem arises when they are called upon to identify their own purpose.

When I first started teaching purpose, people would swarm me when I was done with my presentation, telling me how much it meant to them and asking me questions. I was elated, but then deflated when I would ask them what they thought their purpose was, only to have them respond, "I have no idea" or "I think it's sort of like maybe you know, sort of like to help people, but not me, but God working in and through me." Those general and vague responses drove me to develop all kinds of materials to help people find and fulfill their purpose. This book is the result of that desire.

PurposeCoach was one of those programs I developed. It didn't last very long, because I tried to charge money for it, and I soon discovered most people are addicted to "free." They were not willing to pay very much (if anything) to help them identify their purpose so I discontinued the program after seven lessons. Those lessons included purpose teaching and examples in four areas of life:

1. Purpose in the church
2. Purpose in the marketplace
3. Purpose in the family
4. Personal purpose

In those seven original installments, I included many references, some from my own books (I only had a few at the time) and others from historical and biblical figures who exemplified or modeled purpose. I used case studies and personal stories, and all that has been updated to include in this expanded, twentieth-anniversary edition of *I Wrote This Book on Purpose*. Let's get started.

Purpose in the Church

Did you ever notice that you can do anything in the church as long as it's serving as an usher, working in the nursery, or singing in the choir? How did we lose our sense of creativity in ministry? How did we become so narrow and limited in our palette of ministry colors? In part, this happened because we assumed that only those who derive their income from ministry are truly in ministry, and those are usually pastors, administrators, counselors, or musicians. That leaves everything else for the "non-ministry people to do." Consequently, too many people see themselves as not performing ministry, even though they have important things to do in the church.

The other reason is that we have reduced our vision for church ministry by and large to Sunday services—and maybe a midweek service as well. Unless someone has something that can help those services go more smoothly or increase attendance, we are not quite sure what to do with them. Someone whose purpose is to work with international students, for example, has no place in the church or the church budget, and thus we try to see how we can involve them in something the church really "needs"—like ushers, nursery workers, or choir members. The result has been that the church loses valuable human resources, all because of an incorrect mindset.

PurposeCoach Tips

You already have a ministry, even though you are working outside the church.

If you volunteer to serve in your local church (and you should), don't serve beyond your supply of grace to do so in any area.

If your church cannot recognize or include your purpose expression, then it may be time to find a way to do so. For example, I mentioned international student ministry above. A woman founded her own organization to help those students when her church was not interested in pursuing that outreach with her. She stayed in her church, but she no longer looked to the church as the source of her ministry expression.

CASE STUDY: Consider this case study of Paul (The answers will be at the end of this chapter).

1. What did Paul do for a living? (See Acts 18:3).
2. Who wrote the book of Acts?
3. Do you think it's interesting Paul wrote 13 letters in the New Testament, but never mentioned what he did to make a living?
4. In every letter, however, Paul mentioned what his purpose was (go to Acts 26:9-19 and see if you can describe Paul's purpose in a short phrase. Need more help? Then go to Galatians 2:7).
5. Did the early church support Paul's ministry work to the Gentiles? (see Acts 21:17-26).
6. Need help seeing that Paul mentioned his purpose in every letter? Then check out the list of references at the end of this book.

What is the significance of this study for you? It teaches you *not* to define yourself by what you do to make money. Don't define your purpose by what you do for a living, but what you do that gives you pleasure and brings the greatest results to your investment of time and effort.

If you are a church leader, what can you do to broaden the interpretation and expression of ministry in your church? In chapter four, we will discuss a role that I am calling the "purpose pastor" that will improve any church's ability to be creative in shaping ministries according to the people God has given to any individual church.

Purpose in the Marketplace

It isn't necessary that you work in a church to be a person of purpose. God cares about the whole world and may have something for you to do that has its main expression outside the Church. That doesn't make you a second-class citizen in God's kingdom.

My purpose is to create order out of chaos. I have found I can do that inside or outside the Church, depending on the will of God for any season of my life. For example, I have taught at Kabul University in Afghanistan and Regent University in the United States. In both places, I was fulfilling my purpose. I have consulted for churches, companies, and government agencies. My field of work is wherever there happens to be chaos to which I can bring order.

PurposeCoach Tips

Do you think only those who derive income from a church are in full-time ministry? If so, you need to change your thinking. The word "ministry" simply means service. Therefore, no matter where God directs you to serve, you are in ministry.

We will consider Joseph, David, and Daniel as examples of this important point. Did any of them work in a church, synagogue, or religious organization? The answer, of course, is no.

Did they serve God and mankind? The answer, of course, is yes. Consequently, if "secular" work was good enough for those men, it should be good enough for you. There's no need to pine away for ministry in the Church; you have plenty of ministry to do right where you are in the "secular" world.

CASE STUDY: Read Genesis 37-30 and study the life of Joseph. Answer these questions as you read:

1. Read Psalm 105:5-7. Who sent Joseph to Egypt?
2. What do you think Joseph's purpose was?
3. Why didn't Joseph have the dream Pharaoh had? After all, Joseph had two dreams that showed him his purpose.
4. Was Joseph successful in Egypt? Why or why not?
5. Joseph served in government as an administrator. He still speaks to us today because of what he did and where he did it. How can you leave the same legacy where you work? Do you see your work as holy ground? If not, what do you need to do to get that sense of purpose on your job?

Purpose in the Family

There's no age limit to the discovery and fulfillment of purpose. Do you believe that? If you have children or perhaps you teach them, why not take them through a study of young people who were people of purpose? Who were a few of these young people? How about Joseph, Samuel, David, Daniel, Mary the mother of Jesus, and Jesus Himself? What can you learn from the early years of their lives?

CASE STUDY: Let's consider Joseph once more.

1. How old was he when he had his two dreams?
2. How would you define his purpose from the dreams he had?
3. When did he start fulfilling his purpose: when Pharaoh promoted him or prior to that event?
4. How old was Joseph when Pharaoh promoted him?
5. How old was Joseph when his brothers came and bowed before him in fulfillment of his dreams?
6. How long did he have to walk in faith according to the dreams he had as a young man?
7. How long did he serve from the time Pharaoh promoted him until he died?

PurposeCoach Tips

It's important to help young people understand that they can know and function in their God-assigned purpose *now*, while they continue to grow and develop for their future purpose expressions. There's no need to wait. At the same time, they must understand there is a price to pay for purposeful service. I've found that the greater the purpose, the deeper and longer the preparation time.

I read of a Native American who had a

20-year plan to fulfill his purpose. He then spent an additional seven years after that before he finally launched out to serve his people at the age of 46. Young people need to understand that their purpose power will be enhanced the more developed and prepared they are. Ask the young people with whom you work to think about where they will be and what they will be doing in 20 years. Ask them what they can do today to prepare for that purpose vision. If that man did what he did for his cause, what should and could we do for the cause of Christ?

Personal Purpose

Do you know your purpose? Can you state your purpose in one simple, concise statement? If not, don't worry. That's what this book is designed to help you do. There are no shortcuts to clarify your purpose. You must do the work if you want the results. As your Purpose Coach, it is my job to give you new ways of thinking about and looking at purpose. We have only just begun our quest for purpose. Let's return now to the portion of the book that will help you with develop your personal purpose statement.

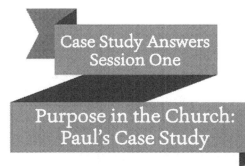

Case Study Answers
Session One

**Purpose in the Church:
Paul's Case Study**

1. What did Paul do for a living? (See Acts 18:3).
   He made tents.

2. Who wrote the book of Acts?
   Luke wrote it.

3. Do you think it's interesting that Paul wrote 13 letters that we have in the New Testament, but never mentioned what he did to make a living?
   The point is that Paul never took his identity from what he did, but rather from his life purpose, which was to take the gospel to the Gentiles. You should do the same.

4. In every letter, however, Paul did mention what his purpose was (go to Acts 26:9-19 and see if you can describe Paul's purpose in a short phrase. Need help? Then go to Galatians 2:7).
   Paul's purpose was to take the gospel to the Gentiles. Notice the minimal effect Paul had among his own people. Even though he loved his fellow Jews, his ministry among them netted meager results. Your purpose is never what you wish it would be, but what God assigned it to be.

Purpose in the Marketplace

Joseph's Case Study

1. Who sent Joseph to Egypt? Read Psalm 105:5-7.

   The Lord sent Joseph to Egypt. In many ways, he was the world's first missionary. Notice what the Lord had in store for Joseph when he got to Egypt—slavery, misunderstanding, temptation, etc. Don't underestimate what God will do to prepare you for His work.

2. What do you think Joseph's purpose was?

   His purpose was to lead his family, as indicated by two dreams in which his family bowed down to him.

3. Why didn't Joseph have the dream Pharaoh had? After all, Joseph had two dreams that showed him his purpose.

   Who would have listened if Joseph had the dream about the coming good and bad years in Egypt? When Pharaoh had the dream, however, everyone had to listen. Sometimes your purpose is only fulfilled in the context of someone else's dream or purpose. They help define who you are and what you are to do.

4. Was Joseph successful in Egypt? Why or why not?

   You would have to say he was successful. He saved the world from famine, enriched Pharaoh in the process, and then was reunited with and thus saved his family.

Joseph fulfilled his purpose and that was what made him successful.

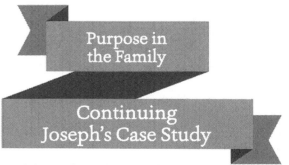

Purpose in the Family

Continuing Joseph's Case Study

1. How old was he when he had his two dreams?
   He was 17 (see Genesis 37:2).
2. How would you define his purpose from the dreams that he had?
   His purpose was to become the leader of his family.
3. When did he start fulfilling his purpose? When he was promoted by Pharaoh or prior to that event?
   Since his preparation commenced right after he had the dreams, Joseph began fulfilling his purpose as a 17-year-old dreamer.
4. How old was Joseph when Pharaoh promoted him?
   He was 30 years of age (see Genesis 41:36). Therefore, he had 13 years of preparation to fulfill his purpose.
5. How old was Joseph when his brothers came and bowed before him in fulfillment of his dreams?
   They came to Joseph and bowed down in the second year of the famine (see Genesis 45:6). Since he was 30 when he took power, and ruled through seven good years and then two years of famine, that made him 39 when his dreams were literally fulfilled.

6. How long did he have to walk in faith according to the dreams that he had as a young man?

   When you do the math, it was 22 years.

7. How long did he serve from the time Pharaoh promoted him until he died?

   He was 30 when he began and died at 110, so he served for 80 years. He endured 13 years of preparation for 80 years of service. Often, the more significant the eventual purpose, the deeper and more intense the required preparation.

CHAPTER 2
Productivity Requires Purpose

"One purpose of life is to discover who we are. Finding out who we are, though, is not as easy as it would seem. We are so much a part of the group that we have to listen very closely to discover our inner self . . . what our uniqueness is. It is when we finally hear the truth of ourselves that we discover our own creativity. This process of self-discovery is as important as the possible products of that discovery." — Joyce Wycoff

When I start an all-day seminar to help people better define their purpose, I often ask the participants to attempt to define it. Some will stare at me, not knowing what to write since no one has ever asked them that question. Others write things like, "To do the will of God," "to worship the Lord," "to glorify God," "to help people," or "to serve mankind." Before we go on, why don't you try to do the same thing? Spend a bit of time in the space below describing your purpose in a short phrase or two.

What is Your Purpose in Life?

_____

_____

_____

_____

The answers that people often give me, while general in nature, aren't really wrong. They simply lack the focus and clarity needed to help them know what it is that constitutes "doing God's will," "worshiping Him," or "bringing Him glory." I've found the words of Jesus helpful in understanding this concept when He said,

> "Father, the time has come. Glorify your Son, that your Son may glorify you. For you have granted him authority over all people that he might give eternal life to all those you have given him. Now this is eternal life: that they may know you, the only true God, and Jesus Christ, whom you have sent. *I have brought you glory on earth by completing the work you gave me to do*" (John 17:1-4, emphasis added).

Jesus brought "glory to God" by completing the work the Father gave Him to do. You will do the same as you find your purpose and make effort to fulfill it.

This isn't always an easy journey to complete and many people shy away from the process, intuitively sensing that it can be a tough and sometimes painful journey of self-analysis and soul-searching. It is also a subjective journey, which means there is no one to tell you that you are finished, you are right or wrong, or it does or does not make sense. I named my company PurposeQuest because the search for purpose is a quest and an ongoing journey to gain clarity as to your purpose statement and how to express it.

Richard Bolles, who has authored the annually updated best-seller, *What Color is Your Parachute?*, writes these words that will encourage you as you search:

> But having to wait for the voice of God to reveal what our Mission is, is not the truest picture of our situation. St. Paul, in Romans, speaks of a law "written in our members,"— and this phrase has a telling application to the question of **how** God reveals to each of us our unique Mission in life. Read again the definition of our third Mission (above) and you will see: the clear implication of the definition is that God has *already* revealed His will to us concerning our vocation and Mission, by causing it to be "*written in our members.*" We are to begin deciphering our unique Mission by studying our talents and skills, and more particularly which ones (or One) we most rejoice to use.
>
> God actually has written His will twice in our members: *first in the talents* which He lodged there, and secondly *in His guidance of our heart*, as to which talent gives us the greatest pleasure from its exercise (*it is usually the one which,*

when we use it, causes us to lose all sense of time).

Even as the anthropologist can examine ancient inscriptions, and divine from them the daily life of a long-lost people, so we by examining *our talents* and *our heart* can *more often than we dream* divine the Will of the Living God. For true it is, our Mission is not something He *will* reveal; it is something He *has already* revealed. It is not to be found written in the sky; it is to be found written in our members (emphasis added).[5]

Recognizing what's already "written in your members" (Romans 7:23) will lead you to happiness and true *effectiveness*, which is defined by *Vine's Dictionary of Old and New Testament Words* as "being full of power to achieve results." You don't want to play at business, school, or church, nor do you want to live out your days staying busy or making money so you can eat and recreate. You should want to get results—the Bible calls it to bear fruit—and you'll get those results most often when you are functioning in your purpose.

Through a failed business opportunity, I discovered in 1981 that my purpose was to **make order out of chaos**. In 2007, I adjusted that statement, replacing the word "make" with the word "create." That was a big step for me because I had often ignored and even denied my creativity, and I came to realize I didn't administrate or organize chaos, I applied my creativity to produce order. There is much more I could explain about that, but my point is that purpose is a process that becomes clearer to you as time goes on, it requires effort to be clear—and then additional effort to get even clearer.

When I am creating order out of chaos, I feel most fulfilled. In keeping with my pattern, I still haven't looked for a job in my entire adult life. My jobs, including my current position or positions, have come to me. I also have the privilege of traveling and helping others find their purpose, not necessarily because I'm a great teacher, but because helping people find purpose is part of my purpose: creating order out of chaos.

This purpose is also consistent with who I am and the gifts and talents I have. I'm organized, focused, disciplined, and task-oriented. I look at the bottom line and I'm practical. The words "order out of chaos" were simply a concise way of describing the gift package and life philosophy that have always been mine.

God wants you to fulfill your purpose more than you do. That's why He created you and the reason you are still here. If you identify, verbalize, and take steps to fulfill your purpose, God will bring more than enough opportunities for you to express it, along with the help to be successful and bear fruit. In fact, you've probably already been expressing your purpose, maybe without realizing it.

Often people come to me and report that they have *no idea* what their purpose is. I say, "None?" and they reply, "Correct." I then ask, "Would you like to drive a big truck?" and they answer no. Then I ask if they would like to be an astronaut or a brain surgeon, and they again say no. My response is that if they had *no* idea, they would have to answer *maybe* to all my questions. The fact that they respond no means that they have *some* idea of what their purpose is. Then I proceed to ask more questions and often they discover what they have been doing but taking for granted is their life purpose. More on that later.

As you can tell, I enjoy reading and studying the Bible. It's a relevant book for modern man, even though some of it was written 4,000 years ago. Let me give you some biblical and modern examples of people who discovered they were doing things "on purpose." Perhaps they will stir your pot or prime your pump so you can identify your own purpose.

Biblical Examples

With a little work and creative imagination, you can identify the life's purpose of anyone in the Bible. I offer the following examples as proof of this statement:

- Jesus – *to seek and save the lost* (see Luke 19:10)
- Adam – *be fruitful, multiply, fill the earth and subdue it* (see Genesis 1:28)
- Eve – *to be a helper suitable to Adam* (see Genesis 2:18)
- Abraham – *to be a great nation* (see Genesis 12:2)
- Joseph – *to rule over his father's sons* (see Genesis 37:8)
- Joshua – *to lead the people into the land* (see Joshua 1:6)

29

- David – *to be king over Israel* (see 1 Samuel 16:12-13)
- Isaiah – *to "go and tell this people"* (see Isaiah 9:6)
- Jeremiah – *be a prophet to the nations* (see Jeremiah 1:5)
- Daniel – *be a source of wisdom, knowledge, and discernment* (see Daniel 2:21)
- John the Baptist – *prepare the way of the Lord* (see Matthew 3:3)
- Mary, Jesus' mother – *believe all the Lord spoke to her* (see Luke 1:45)
- Andrew and Peter – *be fishers of men* (see Matthew 4:19)

See what I mean? Now it's your turn to do some research of your own? See if you can identify and write out the purpose of the person listed below by looking up the reference I provided (at the end of this chapter, I will give you my interpretation of each one's purpose):

Joseph _____

– Genesis 37:8-11

Moses _____

– Acts 7:25; Exodus 2:14

Deborah _____

– Judges 4:4-5, 15

Solomon _____

– 1 Kings 4:29-34, 1:13

Esther _____

– Esther 4:14

Nehemiah_____

– Nehemiah 2:1-20

The Apostle Peter _____

– Matthew 4:18, 16:18-19; Galatians 2:7-8

The Apostle Paul _____

– Acts 26:16-18

Perhaps you are thinking by now: Those were Bible people and it was probably easier for them than it is for me because God spoke to them. What about me? What is my purpose statement? Let's return to *What Color is Your Parachute?* for some practical examples of purpose statements from modern day men and women that will help you in your attempts to define yours.

> Your unique and individual mission will most likely turn out to be a mission of Love, acted out in one or all of three arenas: either in the kingdom of the Mind, whose goal is to bring more Truth into the world; or in the Kingdom of the Heart, whose goal is to bring more beauty into the world; or in the Kingdom of the Will, whose goal is to bring more Perfection into the world, through Service.[6]

Here are some examples:

- "My mission is, out of the rich reservoir of love which God seems to have given me, to nurture and show love to others—most particularly to those who are suffering from incurable diseases."

- "My mission is to draw maps for people to show them how to get to God."

- "My mission is to create the purest foods I can, to help people's bodies not get in the way of their spiritual growth."

- "My mission is the make the finest harps I can so that people can hear the voice of God in the wind."

- "My mission is to make people laugh, so that the travail of this earthly life doesn't seem quite so hard to them."

- "My mission is to help people know the truth, in love, about what is happening out in the world, so that there will be more honesty in the world."

- "My mission is to weep with those who weep, so that in my arms they may feel themselves in the arms of that Eternal Love which sent me and which created them."

- "My mission is to create beautiful gardens, so that in the lilies of the field people may behold the Beauty of God and be reminded of the Beauty of Holiness."

These statements are beautiful expressions of the individuality given to each person by his or her Creator. In those examples, each one had a clear, concise statement summarizing his or her existence. They were specific enough to give direction, but general enough to give room for creative expression. You need that same clarity if you want any chance to be effective and productive. The arenas Bolles created to categorize life purpose or mission can also be quite helpful. They are:

1. Kingdom of the Mind—to bring truth into the world.
2. Kingdom of the Heart—to bring more beauty into the world.
3. Kingdom of the Will—to bring more perfection into the world through service.

In which of those three arenas do you tend to function? As you move toward developing a clear statement and as we close this chapter, it's important that you place yourself in one of those three categories. In chapter five, we will continue the process of finding a statement that describes what is already "written in your members." Before we get there, however, you will have another PurposeCoach session in the next chapter.

(Here is my interpretation of the purpose statement for each of the individuals mentioned earlier in this chapter.)

Joseph: <u>rule over his brothers</u>–Genesis 37:8-11

Moses: <u>rescue his people from Egyptian slavery</u>–Acts 7:25; Exodus 2:14

Deborah: <u>lead her people in troubled times</u>–Judges 4:4-5, 15

Solomon: <u>discover and dispense wisdom</u>–1 Kings 4:29-34, 1:13

Esther: <u>save her people through her beauty</u>–Esther 4:14

Nehemiah: <u>rebuild the city of his fathers</u>–Nehemiah 2:1-20

The Apostle Peter: <u>take the gospel to the Jews</u>–Matthew 4:18, 16:18-19; Galatians 2:7-8

The Apostle Paul: <u>take the gospel to the Gentiles</u>–Acts 26:16-18

Are these summaries "correct"? I am not worried if they are exactly right. What I am looking for is a general summary describing what each person was born to do. You should be looking for the same in your own life. Don't agonize over all the words; find the essence of who you are, put it into words, and then go about doing it more than you are now. You can always tweak or adjust it later. It's more important that you walk in the truth of what you know now than to wait so you can perfect your statement, which is always a work in progress.

PurposeCoach

Session

Two

"Therefore although it be good and profitable that we should ask, and learn and know what good and holy men have wrought and suffered, and how God hath dealt with them, and what he hath wrought in and through them, yet it were a thousand times better that we should in ourselves learn and perceive and understand, who we are, how and what our own life is, what God is and what he is doing in us, what he will have from us, and to what ends he will or will not make use of us. [For, of a truth, thoroughly to know oneself, is above all art, for it is the highest art. It thou knowest thyself well, thou art better and, more praiseworthy before God, than if thou didst not know thyself, but didst understand the course of the heavens and of all the planets and stars, also the virtue of all herbs, and the structure and dispositions of all mankind, also the nature of all beasts, and, in such matters, hadst all the skill of all who are in heaven and on earth. For it is said, there came a voice from heaven, saying, 'Man, know thyself'"—anonymous author of the book Theologia Germanica, 14th century.

Since 1991, I have been helping people all over the world venture out into what I call their PurposeQuest. Little did I know the purpose message would be in such demand today. I am in the right place at the right time with the right message to touch many lives throughout the world, and it has been an exciting journey. As your PurposeCoach, let me guide you through this second session to help you understand how purpose impacts your various roles in life, with the goal of defining your purpose for why you are here.

Purpose in the Church

Most pastors I have worked with aren't interested in the purpose message. I find this intriguing, for my impression was that the pursuit of purpose fit perfectly into the mission statement for pastors and church workers found in Ephesians 4:11-13:

> It was he who gave some to be apostles, some to be prophets, some to be evangelists, and some to be pastors and teachers, to prepare God's people for works of service, so that the body of Christ may be built up until we all reach unity in the faith and in the knowledge of the Son of God and become mature, attaining to the whole measure of the fullness of Christ.

What better preparation for "works of service" can there be than someone fulfilling their purpose? And the success of Rick Warren's book, *The Purpose Driven Life*, indicates that there is tremendous hunger for the purpose message among believers and non-believers alike. Given that fact, I am recommending that every church appoint a purpose pastor. What would this purpose pastor do? I'm glad you asked. Here is my job description for a congregation's purpose pastor:

1. Listen to the members and find out what

the Spirit is saying to as many as possible.

2. Work at getting people involved in the work of the church. This means that new ministries will have to be developed based on the gifts and purpose of the people and not just the vision of the leadership.

3. Recommend books and sponsor seminars to help people know their purpose. This would include personality profiling, spiritual gifts assessments, and purpose-related topics.

4. Then host seminars and lectures to help people fulfill their purpose. This would include sessions on how to start a business, a nonprofit, how to write and publish a book, and missions opportunities available.

5. Make all the leaders in the church aware of what God is doing in the lives of the members so leaders can respond to the agenda of the Holy Spirit as it emerges among the people.

PurposeCoach Tips

If you are a church leader, don't wait for someone to be appointed before you emphasize purpose in the church. Begin to talk about purpose in your youth groups, small

> groups, Bible studies, or church departments.
> The key to helping anyone find their purpose
> is to ask good questions, listen, and then
> give feedback.
> ────────────
> If you are not a church leader, see what you
> can do to emphasize and learn about purpose
> on your own.

CASE STUDY: I think Jesus was an effective purpose coach, don't you? Consider these situations:

1. Jesus found Peter fishing and related Peter's life work to his purpose of being fishers of men (see Mark 4:19).

2. Jesus met a woman at a well as described in John 4. She was living with a man and had been married five times before. Do you think this woman's purpose was to evangelize, but she got sidetracked by her needs to be loved and accepted by men? Study how Jesus led her into a knowledge of who He was and who she was (read John 4). What did she do after that? She evangelized her entire village.

3. Jesus met Saul on the Damascus road (see Acts 9 and 26) and brought Saul face-to-face with his purpose of evangelizing the Gentiles. Jesus did not talk to Saul about sin or repentance; He talked to Saul about purpose. The church would be better off if it spent more time talking about purpose and less talking against sin. Do you agree?

What is the significance of those points for you?

Church should be a place where people find an

expression (or at least encouragement and spiritual training) for their purpose and not only a place where they are kept busy carrying on the traditional ministry projects. That requires creativity and the ability to help people identify who they are and what they were created to do. Perhaps you can begin to help others find and fulfill their purpose. You will find many resources on my website at www.purposequest.com to help you help others be people of purpose.

Purpose in the Marketplace

If you want profitable results in your business, find what people do best and help them do it. You can't get world-class results by sending people to seminars to teach them how to do something. You first find out what they do best (or at least what they are passionate to do, even if they are ill-equipped) and then send them to training that will make them even better. The ideal is to find what someone would do for free and then pay them to do it.

PurposeCoach Tips

Do you think purpose has any place in business? Or is your attitude "this is what I hired you to do, so go do it"?

Are you trying to work with someone in your place of employment who can't do what you want?

Are you falling into the same trap, trying to be diligent in a role in which you are uncomfortable, out-of-place, or unhappy?

There is a book on this subject that you must read or re-read. Its title is *First, Break All the Rules* by Curt Coffman and Marcus Buckingham. The authors reported the results of the Gallup poll of 80,000 managers the world over, so their conclusions are backed by solid research and data. There is a quote from the book I have used again and again. They wrote:

Simply put, this is the one insight we heard echoed by tens of thousands of great managers: People don't change that much. Don't waste time trying to put in what was left out. Try to draw out what was left in. That is hard enough.[7]

One of the chapters in their book is "Talent: How Great Managers Find It." Substitute the word "purpose" for "talent" and it fits right in with this PurposeCoach Tip.

CASE STUDY: Read Exodus 31:1-11 and 35:30–36:1.

1. What did the Spirit enable Bezalel to do?

2. Do you find it interesting that Bezalel had the Spirit of God not to perform "church" duties but rather to work with his hands? Do you know anyone like that? Are you like that? What are you filled with the

Spirit of God to do?

3. Did God have a specific job for Bezalel or was he free to do anything around his workshop?

4. Who was Bezalel's assistant? Did Bezalel "hire" him based on an open position he had in his company or was it a divine appointment based on the assistant's gifts and skill?

5. Who determined what was to be produced and how each person's purpose was to be expressed—the workmen or God?

6. How will reading this change the way your work? Where you work? How will change the way you hire others to work with you?

Purpose in the Family

As I mentioned in the Chapter Two, there's no age limit (young or old) to when someone can discover or fulfill purpose. I have addressed many youth groups, a group with which I don't normally "connect" well. When I speak to them about purpose, however, I find them eager to listen and learn more. If you have children in your family, including nieces and nephews, I urge you to talk to them about purpose. That is not the same as asking them what they want to do when they grow up, but rather questions like, "What do you enjoy doing. What do you feel like you can do well? What are you doing that makes you happiest?"

For example, our two-year old granddaughter loves music. She can clap to the beat of any song, and is happiest when she is watching music videos on her iPad. Our daughter has already enrolled her in weekly music classes. We sing with her when we are in the car. We buy her music-related gifts. We don't know where this is going to end up, but for right now, we are paying attention and music is definitely an interest and may be a gift for her.

Just off the top of your head, can you name young people of purpose in the Bible? Need some help. That's why I'm your Coach! Look at the case study below:

CASE STUDY: Here is a list of young people of purpose from the Bible, some of whom we looked at in the last chapter. Notice how each person was finding or fulfilling purpose at a young age.

1. Joseph: Joseph was 17 when he had his purpose dreams–Genesis 37:1-3

2. Moses: Moses' parents saw purpose in their baby boy–Acts 7:20-23

3. Samuel: Hannah helped guide Samuel's purpose before he was born–1 Samuel 1, 2 and 3

4. David: David was a teenager when he was summoned into royal duty–1 Samuel 16:1-13

5. Daniel: As a youth, Daniel studied and then assumed a significant role in Babylon–Daniel 1

6. John the Baptist: John's parents also knew his purpose before he was born–Luke 1:11-17, 1:44, and 1:76-79

7. Mary: Mary was probably a teenager when she gave birth to Jesus–Luke 1:26-38

PurposeCoach Tips

If God isn't intimidated by or hesitant to use youth, neither should we. I was once with a group of young adults in England whom God was using to plant a church. They didn't need to wait 20 years to be effective; they were being effective at that point in their lives.

Do you know someone young whom you can encourage in his or her purpose?

Are you young and dismissing your usefulness because of your age? Remember what Paul wrote to Timothy:

Flee the evil desires of youth, and pursue righteousness, faith, love and peace, along with those who call on the Lord out of a pure heart (2 Timothy 2:22).

Don't let anyone look down on you because you are young, but set an example for the believers in speech, in life, in love, in faith and in purity (1 Timothy 4:12-13).

Personal Purpose

In Chapter Two, we discussed how to clarify your purpose. After sending these lessons out to subscribers, I got the following statement from someone. I thought she did a good job of coming up with her purpose statement and I share it to help you clarify your own:

I gave my life to Jesus when I was a child

and have been blessed with opportunities to serve Him throughout my life. I am currently employed in a Christian non-profit ministry. Recently through prayer, Scripture, and study; God has shown me that my purpose is to "give confidence to the insecure" within or outside the church of Christ. A verse that helped me identify and express this purpose is found in Ephesians 4:12 "to prepare God's people for works of service, so that the body of Christ may be built up." – CN

Before we move on, let's look at the issue of values. After you find your purpose, it is also important you know your values—what is important to you. For values to be valid, they must appear in two places—your calendar and your checkbook. You must spend time and money on what is important or else you are only talking about what is important and not doing anything about it.

CASE STUDY: To help you think about values and how to define them, I include a few from my study of Paul's life. Can you think of any others?

1. Acts 20:33-35 and 1 Corinthians 9:12: He took no ministry support from churches where he ministered.
2. Romans 15:20: Paul did not minister where others had already been.
3. Acts 13:46: He went to the Jews first on any ministry trip.
4. Acts 13:1; 15:40-41; 16:6-13: Paul always traveled with a team.

Do you see Paul's values governed his life and decisions? What are you values that determine what you will do? Do you know? If you do, then it may be time to review them and see if you are living them out. If not, go to my website, read the article about values found in the Leadership section, and then follow the instructions to write out your own. When you are finished, feel free to send them to me.

This is important because it will help guide you into where and how you should express your purpose. For example, one of my values is reconciliation. I just don't want diverse people to get along or tolerate one another. I want them to put their bitterness and distrust aside and be one in Christ. That value has helped determine where I have gone to church, the college for which I taught, and the work I have done in Africa. My purpose, which is to create order out of chaos, has most often been expressed in our urban communities and in Africa with people who do not look like me.

Another example of how values play a role in purpose is my value of learning. That value led me to earn four graduate degrees and to read or listen to hundreds of books. If learning is truly a value, it will find its expression in my calendar and checkbook—I will spend money and time living it out.

That's it for your PurposeCoach session. Let's move on to the next chapter that will assist you in writing your own statement as we discuss the fact that your purpose is both personal and progressive.

CHAPTER 3

Purpose is Personal and Progressive

Years ago, I was in Wichita, Kansas conducting an all-day purpose seminar. As was my custom, I sent the participants off to lunch with a simple assignment. I asked them to talk to those with whom they had come (who were attending a different seminar than mine) and to return with some idea of how others saw them. I found this often helped my "students" to see their purpose more clearly.

On this particular day, I called on one woman to give me her report and she proceeded to share the following story: "Well, when I asked people what they thought my purpose was, they began to describe me using words like 'joy,' 'rejoicing,' and happiness.' My favorite verse from the Bible is Nehemiah 8:10, which states that 'the joy of the Lord is my [your] strength.' But joy couldn't be my purpose, could it?"

The interesting thing wasn't just what she told me, but how she told it to me. The whole time she was talking in front of the class, she had this huge smile frozen across her face. I asked her what she did in her church and she told me she was the worship leader. I asked her what feedback she got from her leading and she said, "People always tell me they love to watch me, because they feel so uplifted and happy when I sing."

I then said to her jokingly, "I'll bet you hear bad news and it takes you a week to figure out it's bad." She immediately responded that people had accused her of ignoring reality or having her head in the clouds, but then added, "I figure, why let stuff like that get you down?"

Here was a woman whose purpose was to bring the joy of the Lord into any situation in which she found herself. God had given her some part of His own character and personality, so that when people touched her joy, they would actually come in contact with an aspect of God Himself. In a world filled with sadness and grief, that woman's purpose of joy was certain to be in great demand. She left the seminar with a whole new sense of self-awareness and direction. She also realized that if her purpose was to disburse joy, then God was going to send her to people who had little to no joy, and by her own description, that was what had been happening most of her life.

That's how your purpose is. It's what I call personal. The Lord can take a simple phrase, mentioned by someone else or in the Bible, and quicken it to you so it brings you much-needed definition and understanding. While others can hear that word or phrase and it not mean anything to them, for you that word becomes personal because it defines why you were born and why you are still here.

Once you see that word of purpose, it will become clearer to you over time just how significant it is and how you can use it to serve God and be effective. That's why I also say it's progressive. Look at what Paul wrote about the progressive nature and understanding of his purpose:

> I did not receive it [the gospel to the Gentiles] from any man, nor was I taught it; rather, I received it by revelation from Jesus Christ...But when God, who set me apart from birth and called me by his grace, was pleased to reveal his Son in me so that I might preach him among the Gentiles, I did not consult any man, nor did I go up to Jerusalem to see those who were apostles before I was, ...Then after three years, I went up to Jerusalem to get acquainted with Peter and stayed with him fifteen days. . . . Fourteen years later I went up again to Jerusalem, this time with Barnabas, . . . and set before them the gospel that I preach among the Gentiles. . . .They saw that I had been entrusted with the task of preaching the gospel to the Gentiles, just as Peter had been to the Jews (Galatians 1:12, 15-16, 18, 2:1-2, 7).

Even though Paul had a dramatic encounter

during which his purpose was revealed to him (see Acts 26:9-19), he still experienced a progressive understanding of what he was to do and how he was to do it as his life and ministry went on. Even though he had companions on that road who saw the light and knew that something had happened, only Saul heard the voice and knew what it meant. He had a personal encounter and his comprehension of the significance of that encounter grew over time.

As I've worked with people to help them find their purpose, I've seen some powerful encounters as individuals have come to know their personal purpose. I've then watched them make progress as they've seen just what the Lord had in mind when He assigned them their purpose. Let me give you a few examples.

Dr. Reggies

In 1995, I was visiting Zimbabwe and had the opportunity to conduct a seminar on finding your purpose. Reggies Wenyika, a young salesman for a medical company, attended the seminar, heard my purpose message, and was stirred by what he heard. He earnestly sought the Lord for clarity so he could know his purpose. He came to the conclusion that his purpose was to "bring them in, raise and train them to bring others in." Realizing the full impact of what this would mean for the rest of his life, he had a rubber stamp made with his purpose statement and proceeded to stamp his purpose in his Bible and on other possessions. From there, he made the decision to leave the medical company and enter into full-time ministry as a youth worker at his local church in his native land.

Throughout this time, Reggies attended a local Bible college. He continued to seek clarity as to how he could translate his purpose statement into a clear road map for the future. He received his bachelor's degree in biblical studies in 1998 and had a sense that his purpose was somehow related to higher education. Based on that intuitive sense and the realization that he needed to further his education in preparation for this, Reggies set the wheels in motion and moved his young family to the United States where he enrolled at Oral Roberts University and earned his master's and doctorate in education. He also earned a Master of Ministry degree in leadership from Southwestern Christian University.

Fulfilling one's purpose is a marathon and not a sprint and Dr. Reg's journey continued. At first, he served as an instructor, before becoming an administrator, an academic dean, provost, and then the twelfth president of Southwestern Christian University in Oklahoma City. When his tenure ended there, he moved on to another college presidency, and as we publish in 2018, he is the president at Ottawa University in Ottawa, Kansas. He has also traveled extensively in ministry, speaking to crowds, all the while being true to his purpose, which is finding, training, and then releasing people the world over who in turn will find others with whom they can do the same.

Irene

It is my custom in the countries I visit to make

myself available for one-on-one purpose coaching sessions. In Kenya, hundreds of people have taken me up on my offer, and it is not unusual to meet with 25 to 30 people in a two-week period. On one visit, I was staying at the Nairobi Hilton where I met with Irene, who worked in a bank but was also disconnected from any sense of purpose. As usual, I started out with a battery of personality assessments to get to know the person with whom I was meeting, and Irene profiled to be an outgoing, creative entrepreneur. That led me to ask her, "What are you doing in a bank?"

That question triggered a waterfall of tears during which Irene told me how unhappy she was and how she felt like she was dying. I did not tell her what to do, but I told her there was so much more to her than what she was doing, and we parted ways. Before long, Irene had started her own coaching service to help others find their purpose. She now administers the profiles I first used with her. She lectures, writes, and coaches people about how they can become a person of purpose like she is. She almost always has me address her clients and students when I return to Kenya.

Yvonne

In 2001, my wife and I traveled to Birmingham England at the invitation of Yvonne Brooks and her pastor husband, Melvin. Yvonne had heard my purpose message the previous year while I was in London, and was impressed that I was to come to Birmingham to expose the church and her friends to the purpose message.

We had a wonderful time during that first visit and became quite close. Yvonne already had an organization called Women in the Word, but the purpose message touched her so deeply that eventually she changed the name of the organization to Women of Purpose. They have held an annual conference for 21 years and many women have been impacted by the purpose message. I had the privilege of speaking at a few of the conferences and many of the women I met there still follow me on social media. Yvonne herself was in the mental health field when we met, but today she is in full-time ministry along with her husband who is now Bishop Melvin Brooks. This is how Yvonne defines her purpose: "I am a leader using empathy creativity and humor to draw out the best in people allowing them to see their hidden potential and possibilities."

Glenn

I cannot claim much involvement in this next profile, but I have witnessed the purpose progression of my friend and colleague Glenn over the last 40 years. After a prolonged effort to further an entrepreneurial dream, Glenn had to move into the construction and building business to support his family. He obtained his degree in his early fifties and then transitioned into ministry at the age of 55. Today, he leads a growing and influential foreign missions movement at a local church, mentoring and training many candidates for deployment in the field. My publishing company just completed a book for Glenn and he has several more publishing ideas to pursue. Now in his sixties, Glenn is traveling and enjoying his purpose life, which took a while to emerge but has made a significant impact since he embraced his purpose to the nations.

John

All right, I was going to make this profile anonymous or third person, but it won't work. This is my purpose progress story, which I have shared with audiences the world over. In 1991, I found through a failed business opportunity that my purpose is to "create order out of chaos." I didn't know what that meant for my future, but I knew it was something I had always done—take a new position or challenge, structure it, and then move on.

For the next 10 years, I served in a variety of positions in a local church. In 1989, I first taught a seminar on how to find purpose in, of all places, a federal penitentiary. In 1991, I had the chance to teach the same class as I traveled with Ron (mentioned above) and the others in the music company to conduct church music seminars. The response was so positive and overwhelming when I taught on purpose that I began to expand my repertoire of purpose presentations. In 1995, I wrote my first book that included a section on purpose. My second book was the original *I Wrote This Book on Purpose . . . So You Can Know Yours,* the precursor to the expanded version you are currently reading.

In 2001, I started my consulting and coaching company called PurposeQuest Inc. along with my website purposequest.com. In 2004, I founded a nonprofit organization called PurposeQuest International. I also began writing and distributing, *The Monday Memo*, a weekly email exhortation that equips people to be more purposeful (as of this writing, I have published 880 *Memos*). I have met with thousands of people in private purpose coaching sessions and thousands more in seminars, workshops, and preaching engagements. What started as a simple epiphany after the business failed turned into a worldwide purpose movement I helped launch. That is the power of a personal purpose realization that grew as time went on.

I have founded two companies with the name PurposeQuest in their moniker. I wish I could say that combination of purpose and quest came after much seeking and searching—but it did not. In 1998 when I was starting a website, I was asked to come up with a domain name. After finding that my first five or six choices were already taken, I asked the designer, "How about PurposeQuest?" and it was available. There were no focus groups or brainstorming sessions. I look back on that christening, and it was a profound moment, for purpose is indeed a quest (I combined the two words to help brand my unique purpose presentation).

When it came time to choose a logo, I chose a simple outline sketch of several mountains in blue and green. The quest is like climbing a mountain, which the climber must do one step at a time, while taking precautions not to fall back or lose momentum. Purpose is progressive, just like a mountain-climbing expedition, and every step of the quest brings the seeker closer to the summit, which in the case of purpose is both clarity and expression (we will discuss the fruit of purpose in chapter five).

How about you? Do you have a simple, yet profound and personal phrase or statement summarizing your life and existence? Is the statement something that sounds good but has no proof in practical experience, or have you seen it progressively unfold in your life? Are you willing to pay a price to see that purpose statement take root and grow into something bigger than you ever imagined? If you don't have one yet, don't despair. Purpose is a quest, and if you don't give up, you will find what you are looking for.

The culmination of every example of a purpose person in this chapter is that their purpose was not just a statement or platitude, but a life direction and energy that led them to bear fruit—something tangible from which others could benefit. This is what I call purpose proof—the productivity that can only come from knowing and doing (or living) your purpose. With that in mind, let's move on to the next important chapter after another PurposeCoach session.

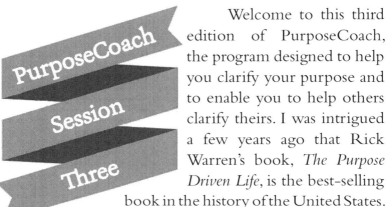

PurposeCoach Session Three

Welcome to this third edition of PurposeCoach, the program designed to help you clarify your purpose and to enable you to help others clarify theirs. I was intrigued a few years ago that Rick Warren's book, *The Purpose Driven Life*, is the best-selling book in the history of the United States.

What does that tell you about the hunger people have for purpose material? Recently, Rick re-released that book under a new name, and it is selling well again. Yet many read the book and, while recognizing they have a purpose, still don't know what that specific purpose is. That's where PurposeQuest and PurposeCoach come in.

Since 1991, I have been helping people all over the world venture out into what I call their PurposeQuest. Little did I know that the purpose message would be in such demand today. I feel like I am in the right place at the right time with the right message.

So as your PurposeCoach, let's dive into this next lesson.

Purpose in the Church

The Apostle Paul wrote, "For we are God's work-manship, created in Christ Jesus to do good works, which God prepared in advance for us to do" (Ephesians 2:10).

Most define "good works" as any act of mercy or

kindness one can do for the benefit of someone else. That is a good definition, but in the context of purpose, I wonder if it is the best definition. Did Paul do good works, or did he do good works designed for him to do? The best "good works" you can do are works related to who you are and what you do best.

Therefore, churches should not only be interested in getting people to do good things leadership has decided need to be done. Instead, leadership should also work to ensure that, more often than not, people are doing good works consistent with a person's purpose and giftedness. Let me give you an example.

Years ago, my wife's sister took a spiritual gifts profile. The profile showed she had gifts of missions and hospitality. She began to prepare for the missions field, but the Lord spoke to her that He wasn't sending her anywhere. She was living in south Alabama with gifts of hospitality and missions but she had nowhere to go—or so she thought.

At that point, she went to the local university to meet the foreign students there. Before long, she found out how lonely they were and befriended them. She approached the university with a plan and became an official host for foreign students. Then she got other families from our church involved. So far, so good.

Eventually, she made a proposal to the church leadership that this program be sponsored and funded by the church. Now that presented a bit of a problem. This proposal didn't come from leadership; it came from among the people. What would the leaders do? To their credit, they adopted and funded the program and it became a model program for other churches. What points am I making here?

1. Foreign students were the good works my sister-in-law was to perform.
2. The church found a way to incorporate her good works into the life of the church, devoting energy and money to the effort.
3. The church grew because my sister-in-law was fulfilling her purpose.

PurposeCoach Tips

What good works were you created to do?

What good works were the others in your church created to do?

Once you find these works, pray for creative ways to express them in your church. If you can't find a way or aren't permitted, then don't use the church as an excuse to do nothing. Find a place to express those good works.

That does not mean you should leave your church; perhaps you can start your own business or nonprofit organization, or simply find a place to volunteer.

If you are in church leadership, identify the gifts and good works of the people around you

and do your best to help them find strategies
to do those good works.

CASE STUDY: Read Acts 9:36-42.

1. What good works was Dorcas created to do?

2. How did those good works impact her church?

3. What happened when she died? What did the church feel?

4. What happened when Dorcas came back to life? How did so many people come to know Jesus? Did she have to preach a sermon for people to come to the Lord?

5. How can you take the lessons from Dorcas' life and apply them to your own? To your church?

Purpose in the Marketplace

I once heard a lecture by Marcus Buckingham, who co-authored the book, *First, Break All the Rules* (mentioned earlier). If you haven't read this book, you need to do so (along with any of the others that Buckingham has written). In the lecture, Buckingham talked about a Gallup survey that asked people, "Are you engaged at work?" The question was designed to measure whether people were doing what they do best on a regular basis. The responses were revealing.

Americans led the survey when 29% responded that they were. That is less than one-third of the workforce, but it went downhill from there. Only 17% of British workers said yes, 9% of Japanese workers, 6% of

French workers, and only 4% of workers in Singapore could say yes to the survey question.

Can you imagine what this means to workplace creativity and productivity? How many people are just reporting for work, leaving the best parts of them in the car or on the bus on their way to work. If you are in leadership, what can you do to assess how engaged your people are? Gallup has a list of 12 questions you can ask people to determine how engaged they are:

The Gallup Q12 Index

Gallup's employee engagement work is based on more than 30 years of in-depth behavioral economic research involving more than 17 million employees. Through rigorous research, Gallup has identified 12 core elements—the Q12—that link powerfully to key business outcomes. These 12 statements emerged as those that best predict employee and workgroup performance. The Twelve Questions are:

1. Do you know what is expected of you at work?
2. Do you have the materials and equipment to do your work right?
3. At work, do you have the opportunity to do what you do best every day?
4. In the last seven days, have you received recognition or praise for doing good work?
5. Does your supervisor, or someone at work, seem to care about you as a person?
6. Is there someone at work who encourages your development?

7. At work, do your opinions seem to count?
8. Does the mission/purpose of your company make you feel your job is important?
9. Are your associates (fellow employees) committed to doing quality work?
10. Do you have a best friend at work?
11. In the last six months, has someone at work talked to you about your progress?
12. In the last year, have you had opportunities to learn and grow?[8]

PurposeCoach Tips

Reflect on these questions and ask yourself what you can do to be more engaged at work. Is it worth the trouble and effort to be engaged at work? If you are in leadership, what can you do to help yourself and others? If you're not a leader, what are willing to do to be engaged?

In chapter three, I quoted from *First, Break All the Rules* and I include the quote one more time for your review.

Simply put, this is the one insight we heard echoed by tens of thousands of great managers: People don't change that much. Don't waste time trying to put in what was left out. Try to draw out what was left in. That is hard enough.

Purpose in the Family

It may not be close to Christmas as you read this, but let's look at the issue of family purpose in the Christmas story and go right to our case study for this lesson.

CASE STUDY: Read Luke 1, which contains the story of Zechariah, Elizabeth, and the birth of John the Baptist. Then answer the following questions:

1. What did the angel reveal to Zechariah about his son's purpose?
2. Do you think it's possible for parents to have divine revelation concerning the purpose of their children, even before they are born?
3. Do you think this revelation is only for children who will work in what we now call "the ministry"?
4. When you read the prayer at the end of the chapter, what did Zechariah say about his son's purpose? Was it more than the angel told him? Do you think those nine months of silence increased his understanding of John's purpose?
5. If Zechariah was quiet for nine months and increased his insight, do you think there is a role for silence in our families as we seek the Lord for one another's purpose?

PurposeCoach Tips

Family is the ideal nurturing ground for purpose. What can you do to promote purpose thinking in your home?

If you're not married, do you have nieces or nephews for whom you can do this?

How about the youth group at your church?

Look at Proverbs 22:6 from the perspective of purpose: *Train a child in the way he should go, and when he is old he will not turn from it* (Proverbs 22:6). This verse not only pertains to moral training, but also to a life purpose path for each child. This requires different thinking than helping them find a job or career because it is about purpose, the essence of who the child is.

Do you see that John's parents raised him in the way he should go and when he was old he did not depart from it? That is what we need to do for our children as well.

Personal Purpose

How is your own PurposeQuest coming along? If you still don't have the clarity that you want, relax. You can't force God to give you anything you're not ready to receive. Keep preparing the soil of your mind and heart to recognize purpose by changing the way you think. Why is that important?

Being a person of purpose requires transformation to take place in your life. You must think new thoughts if you are going to see and do new things. Paul was clear about this in Romans 12:1-2 when he wrote,

Therefore, I urge you, brothers and sisters, in

view of God's mercy, to offer your bodies as a living sacrifice, holy and pleasing to God—this is your true and proper worship. Do not conform to the pattern of this world, but be transformed by the renewing of your mind. Then you will be able to test and approve what God's will is—his good, pleasing and perfect will.

Purpose isn't about what you do—it's about who you are that causes you to do what you do. Purpose requires a different way of thinking so you can comprehend what you will eventually see. People ask me when they find their purpose, "What should I do now?" My stock answer is, "Nothing!" God is more motivated to see you fulfill your purpose than you are, so He will bring the fulfillment to you in most cases. You must only be aware of what it is and prepare by obtaining skills and experience, and then you will recognize the opportunities when they come.

I am 68 years of age as I write and I don't have a resume. I have never looked for a job in my life and I haven't been unemployed for one minute. I've never had to go looking for purpose; it's always come looking for me.

Therefore, don't give up, for you have a ways to go before you finish this book. In fact, while you're searching, why not help others with their PurposeQuest? Consider starting a Bible study or purpose awareness group with a friend or a small group.

You can use any of the case studies in this book or

refer to the list of every Bible verse that mentions purpose, purposes, or purposed in the Appendix. You may want to use the list for personal study or read it once and see if anything draws your interest. If you don't look at anything else, may I recommend my favorite on the list? It is Psalm 138:6-8 in the New American Standard Version. That passage says, "The Lord will accomplish what concerns me." If purpose is your concern, then God will provide the awareness of it and the understanding of how to fulfill it.

Let's get back to our discussion of purpose in the next chapter, which will help you identify your purpose fruit as a source of defining your purpose.

CHAPTER 4
Purpose Demands Proof

I'm sure you have noticed that every chapter title contains a word that begin with the letter "p." We have seen that productivity is a priority, that productivity requires you to function in your purpose, and that purpose is personal and progressive The remaining chapters that are not PurposeCoach sessions will continue this same pattern. I'm not sure why I did this, except that it was fun and a challenge. Remember, my purpose is to create order out of chaos, even if I have to create the chaos to begin with. In this chapter, we will discuss the fact that purpose demands proof.

My quest to understand my purpose began in 1991 in my office in Mobile, Alabama (after a failed business opportunity) when I thought of a verse from the Bible. Genesis 1:2 states, "Now the earth was formless and empty, darkness was over the surface of the deep, and the Spirit of God was hovering over the waters." It was my research of the verse that led me to identify the phrase "order out of chaos" as my life's purpose.

That phrase has progressively unfolded its meaning as I've come to understand the Hebrew concept for chaos isn't confusion and disorder, but includes the concept of potential. I have had the opportunity through my seminars around the world to help many bring order to their potential found in their purpose. I also discovered that once people overcame their fears or misgivings about purpose, a release of their creativity was not far behind, which is why I founded a publishing company to help people express their creative purpose and tell their stories.

My first purpose clue came from the Bible and Genesis 1:2. I stated in the Introduction that our Designer or Creator holds the keys to understanding our purpose. The focal point for God's revelation to man is the Bible, so I expect that "living and active" book to help bring definition to God's creatures. Plus, I have heard pastors say, "The Bible is the oldest book written whose author is still alive." This very-much-alive Author can and does orchestrate this process and His help is our hope to find and fulfill our purpose to the fullest.

People who have heard me give my public presentation about purpose listen to me talk about Jesus' purpose, which is found in the story of Zacchaeus in Luke 19. As Jesus came into Jericho with His entourage, He called that short man down from his vantage point in the sycamore tree. The entire group went to Zacchaeus' home for a meal, at which point the host announced his shocking news: "Look, Lord! Here and now I give half of my possessions to the poor, and if I have cheated anybody out of anything, I will pay back four times the amount" (Luke 19:8).

Jesus replied, "Today salvation has come to this house, because this man, too, is a son of Abraham. For the Son of Man came *to seek and to save what was lost*" (Luke 19:9, emphasis added). Those words represent Jesus' life purpose as well as anything He ever said. More on that practical (another word that begins with "p") aspect of purpose in a later chapter.

Even Jesus had biblical "evidence" or proof for His purpose. To see what it was, we need only look earlier in Luke's gospel:

> He went to Nazareth, where he had been brought up, and on the Sabbath day he went into the synagogue as was his custom. And he stood up to read. The scroll of the prophet Isaiah was handed to him. Unrolling it, he found the place where it is written: 'The Spirit of the Lord is on me, because he has anointed me to preach good news to the poor. He has sent me to proclaim freedom for the prisoners and recovery of sight for the blind, to release the oppressed, to proclaim the year of the Lord's favor.' Then he rolled up the scroll, gave it back to the attendant and sat down. The eyes of everyone in the synagogue were fastened upon him, and he began by saying to them, "Today this scripture is fulfilled in your hearing" (Luke 4:14–21).

This passage Jesus read is from Isaiah 61:1-2. How beautifully and accurately those verses describe what we know of Jesus' earthly ministry expressing His purpose "to seek and save what was lost." Not only was Jesus clear on what He was to do, He was clear on the biblical description and authorization for what He was doing.

Jesus was not alone in having a biblical perspective for His purpose. When the Pharisees pressed John the Baptist for an answer to the question, "Who are you?", he responded by saying, "I am the voice of one calling in the desert, 'Make straight the way of the Lord'" (John 1:23). John was referring to Isaiah 40:3, and somewhere and somehow, the Lord had made that verse a personal "motto" for this great prophet.

When Paul and Barnabas were on their first missions journey, they were preaching in a synagogue in Pisidian Antioch and were challenged by unbelieving and jealous Jews. This was their response:

> Then Paul and Barnabas answered them boldly: "We had to speak the word of God to you first. Since you reject it and do not consider yourselves worthy of eternal life, we now turn to the Gentiles. For this is what the Lord has commanded us: *'I have made you a light for the Gentiles, that you may bring salvation to the ends of the earth.'"* When the Gentiles heard this, they were glad and honored the word of the Lord; and all who were appointed for eternal life believed (Acts 13:46-48, emphasis added).

Paul and Barnabas were quoting Isaiah 49:6. Obviously, they had seen the truth in the Old Testament that the gospel was to be taken to the Gentiles. While others read that verse and were unaffected, Paul and Barnabas saw it and "knew" it to be more than just a distant truth with no meaning for them personally. It was the very reason for their existence and biblical proof for their purpose.

What is your life-defining verse, passage, chapter, or book from the Bible? Often people will refer to something as a favorite verse or passage, but it may be more. Could it hold a clue to your purpose? I challenge you to search and find your life's passage and identify it so it can fit alongside your purpose statement. You aren't looking for something that sounds spiritual or that you think is what you *should* express as a believer. You are looking for something accurately describing what you do and who you are.

I mentioned at the start of this chapter how I was involved in a failed business opportunity that cost me a lot of time and money. One morning, I was praying, rather I was *begging* God to save the business, which He chose not to do. As I prayed, I asked, "If You did not create me to do this business, what *did* You create me to do?" Keep in mind, I was not looking for information, I was frustrated and taking the opportunity to vent my anger toward the Lord.

It was after I asked the question that my mind went to Genesis 1:2. I had not been reading or studying that chapter or verse, so I thought it unusual and assumed it was an answer to my question—the question for which I was not really seeking an answer. Before I explain what I learned about myself from Genesis 1:2, let me remind you about the truth found in James 1:5-8:

> If any of you lacks wisdom, you should ask God, who gives generously to all without finding fault, and it will be given to you. But when you ask, you must believe and not doubt, because the one who doubts is like a wave of the sea, blown and tossed by the wind. That person should not expect to receive anything from the Lord. Such a person is double-minded and unstable in all they do.

When you are seeking answers for purpose—or anything for that matter—you must ask in faith and believe God is able to answer without allowing interference from any outside sources, including the noise in your own mind. If God does not reveal His will to you when you ask, then you are in trouble, for He is expecting you to do something He desires with no input from Him. That is both ludicrous and impossible.

Now, let's go back to Genesis 1:2, which reads, "Now the earth was formless and empty, darkness was over the surface of the deep, and the Spirit of God was hovering over the waters. Someone once told me that his purpose and, as far as he was concerned, *everyone's* purpose was to lead people to Jesus. I agree that the ultimate goal God has for us is to fulfill His desire that "all men to be saved and to come to a knowledge of the truth" (1 Timothy 2:4). When I pressed him, however,

I discovered this man had not led anyone to the Lord for a long time. I wanted to know where his practical evidence was of this purpose he claimed so confidently. After I responded, he got angry and went away feeling, I suppose, that I was teaching error.

My point is this: Your purpose is more than a spiritual platitude or general concept. You should see fruit in the area you claim is your purpose. Jesus had practical evidence to go with his verse and purpose statement. Consider the story in John 4 of the woman at Jacob's well. Jesus was resting at the well while His disciples went to get food. He did not go out and look for the lost; in this instance, the lost came to Him. The crowds consistently sought Him because they were lost and seeking the comfort and direction only a shepherd could give them. That's how it is with purpose.

What group of people consistently seeks you for help? What business opportunities constantly find you, even when you're not looking for them? What effect have you brought to your work, family, ministry, or chance meetings with people on a regular basis? Answers to those questions can help you understand your purpose. There is always evidence to go with a purpose, even before you can recognize or define your purpose. I was creating order out of chaos long before I understood my purpose was to do it.

John the Baptist had this kind of purpose evidence. He was to "make straight the way of the Lord." What did John do to bring this about? He went into the desert where no one else lived, had a wardrobe that no one else shared, ate food that no one else ate, and preached a message that no one else liked. You might say he was a bit eccentric. Yet the entire nation turned out to see and hear him, even those who didn't care for his message. Many did prepare their hearts for the messenger who was to follow John because of John's preaching, and those people were his purpose evidence. God was with him when he made straight the way of the Lord.

Let's consider the life of Saul or the Apostle Paul. He took a message of the covenant that had been the exclusive property of the Jews and carried it to the Gentile nations of the earth. He came unannounced and had to work with idolaters and those who had no Old Testament experience or heritage like Paul did, yet look what happened. Everywhere Paul went, he left a church made up of believers who were from Jewish and Gentile backgrounds. Then he wrote 13 letters, leaving a body of material that would impact the Gentile world for centuries to come. That's the evidence Paul was born to preach the gospel to the Gentiles. When he did, God was with him and there was fruit and confirming evidence that he was on the right path.

Jesus gave Peter the keys to the Kingdom. Until he put the key in the Kingdom lock and turned it, so to speak, the door remained closed. Therefore, Peter was the one who stood up on the day of Pentecost as described in Acts 2 and thousands came to the Lord. He did the same thing as Luke reported in Acts 4. Then Peter went to Cornelius' house and told him how "God anointed Jesus of Nazareth with the Holy Spirit and power, and how he went around doing good and healing all who were under the power of the devil, *because God was with him*" (Acts 10:38, emphasis added). Peter produced fruit consistent with his purpose to be the keeper of the keys of the Kingdom.

It is time to ask yourself, "What is God with me to do?" For example, do people compliment you on your hospitality and ability to make people feel at home? Do you then dismiss it by saying, "Yes, my grandmother owned a restaurant and I used to work there during my summer vacations, but that's not spiritual. If I could only sing like Amy Grant, then God could really use me."? Do people tell you that you have a way of finding mechanical problems and fixing them, only to hear you respond, "Well, my dad had a workshop and we used to work in it together, but that's nothing. I've always been good at that. If I could only preach like Billy Graham, then God could really use me."

Or do folks tell you you're easy to talk to and they feel comfortable sharing their life story and even their secrets with you? Do you say in response, "Oh, my aunt was a polite person and taught me how to listen to people and act like I'm interested, but if I could only help the poor like Mother Teresa, then God could really use me."

I've got news for you. If you fit into any of the above categories or have a similar category, God is already using you—and wants to use you more. Don't look for the hard thing, the super-spiritual thing, or the thing you *think* God and others want you to do or be. Look for the evidence, both biblical or practical, and ask God to show you who you are. If it's good enough for Him, shouldn't it be good enough for you? If it's important to Him that He created you as you are, shouldn't it be important to you?

Don't let the seeming difficulty of finding your purpose stop you from trying. After all, doesn't every servant have the right to know the will of the master. If God wants you to do His will—and He does—He must show you what it is or He can't expect you to do it. We know that He *will* show us if we ask Him—and keep on asking. My job it prepare you so you will recognize what He shows you as you examine your past, your fruit, and your feedback from others. To prepare you, it's time for another PurposeCoach session.

PurposeCoach

Session

Four

Why do you need a purpose coach? You need one because purpose requires you to think different thoughts than you are accustomed to. You have been trained to find out what you are to do in life, and that is usually defined as a job or career. People become doctors, engineers, truck drivers, and teachers. There is nothing wrong with any of those activities but they may not be purpose-driven. Someone could have gone into those activities to make money or because there were job openings and the future looked bright for ongoing employment.

Purpose requires you to think not about what you would do to make money or what your culture honors, but rather about the essence of who you are. You may love to draw or paint, but you know (or have been conditioned to think) you cannot make a living doing that, so you relegate your art to a hobby—if even that. You thought about doing missions work but then got married and had children, so that work is scratched off your list. Yet your art or your missions work, just to continue those two examples, may actually be your purpose and your job or career are to support that work. You see what I mean now that purpose requires you to look at yourself, your life, and your work differently.

The gravitational pull of answering "How will I do that? How will I make money?" is almost impossible to overcome, which is why you need a coach to keep you focused on what you were created to do and not what you see is possible to do. Since I can't be with you, I am including my most common coaching lessons for you to read and apply in this expanded version of *I Wrote This Book on Purpose*. Now that I have explained that, let's move into your next coaching session.

Purpose in the Church

Jesus came preaching the kingdom of God, not the church of God. When you preach the Kingdom, the result is the church. When you preach the church, the result is religion. If people are in a church because it has the best music or they like the schedule of Sunday meetings, they are there for the wrong reasons. They should be present because it is God's will, which is an expression of His kingdom. If the King sent them there, they will stay and serve for the right reasons. If they are there for the same reasons they would join a club—personal preferences or tradition—then they will follow the rules of the church instead of the directives of the King. When the music or the schedule changes, they will leave because what got them to the church will keep them in the church.

How can we define the kingdom of God? The best definition I ever heard was the Kingdom is God's government. What better way to express His government in your life than to find and fulfill your purpose.

If the premise is true that when you preach the Kingdom, you get the Church, and if it's true that your purpose is an expression of the Kingdom, then the Church should be preaching and teaching about purpose. Yet how many messages have you ever heard (or preached) about purpose? What programs or assistance does your church have in place to help someone find and clarify their purpose?

What can be done in the church (or more specifically, in *your* church) to heighten purpose awareness and help people focus on their purpose? May I recommend a few things:

1. Host a purpose seminar where the topic of purpose is taught and discussed, with helpful tips for those present to help them produce a simple purpose statement.

2. Host a seminar for those who have never taken a gift or personality profile. There are many good profiles on the market today. While these don't address the issue of purpose directly, they help people understand themselves better. They also help people talk about who they are (and who they are not), something which is difficult for many to do. This will make it easier for people to continue to talk about themselves as they seek to understand who they are and what they do that bears fruit in their lives and serves others.

3. If the church has a cell or small group meeting structure, use that format to talk about purpose over an extended period.

Members can help others find their purpose and then hold each one accountable for the results and conclusions they find.

4. Teach on purpose from the pulpit or in other settings: staff meetings, choir rehearsals, Bible studies, or retreats.

5. Appoint a purpose pastor or purpose committee with the sole objective of promoting purpose "health" in the congregation. This person or team would make sure that purpose is kept before the congregation and report back to leadership concerning those in the church who are making progress. The purpose pastor or team would then help leadership develop strategies for how to release people into purpose and how the church could benefit from these purpose-full members.

PurposeCoach Tips

You don't have to be the pastor to promote purpose in your church. First, pray and then find creative ways to express your purpose in your church. If you are in some aspect of church leadership, pray and apply purpose principles in your department, team, or committee. Don't wait for someone else to do it. Gandhi said, "We must become the change

> we seek." Follow that advice and do what you
> can where you are to promote purpose.

CASE STUDY: Read Acts 16:1-5, 17:14-15, and Philippians 2:19-23. For this chapter's case study, consider Timothy, Paul's faithful assistant. Timothy wasn't a strong or dominant person. We know this because Paul wrote him on two occasions and urged him to be more assertive, which didn't seem to be in Timothy's nature. Timothy was, however, a faithful "number two" man, able to take the churches Paul started to the next level in their development.

Every church has some Timothys—people who have great potential but need to be teamed with others for greater effectiveness. Can you help find those Timothys? Could you be one yourself? Now, reflect on these questions based on this case study's readings.

1. What do you think Timothy's purpose was?
2. How did Paul utilize him most effectively?
3. According to Philippians 2:19-23, how did Timothy prepare to fulfill his purpose?
4. Did Timothy have to go looking for his purpose or did it (along with its fulfillment) come looking for him?
5. How did Timothy's purpose help the church to grow? What are the lessons you can apply to your own life, purpose, and church?

Purpose in the Marketplace

Some business books on the market today address

the topic of purpose. Why? They do so because purpose is good business. The companies that know their purpose and how to use people of purpose to achieve the company's overall purpose are successful. It's that simple.

While there are many new books that focus on purpose, I still refer to a classic written by the late Stephen Covey. After the release of his best-selling *The 7 Habits of Highly Effective People*, in 1987, he wrote a follow up titled *The 8ᵗʰ Habit*. The eighth habit, according to Covey, was about purpose.

To be specific, Covey defines the eighth habit as "finding your voice and helping others to find theirs." He may use the term voice, but he was really talking about purpose. Purpose is what makes you unique and gives you a special "sound" that attracts others when you express it.

I've taught Covey's *Seven-Habits* material many times, and I thought it would be good to review the seven habits here. They are:

1. Be Proactive
2. Begin with the End in Mind.
3. Put First Things First
4. Think Win/Win
5. Seek First to Understand, Then to Be Understood
6. Synergize
7. Sharpen the Saw

For this session, let's look at *Habit Two: Begin with the End in Mind*. As part of this habit, Covey urged his readers to write their funeral eulogy—the exact remarks they would want others to make when they die. What was the purpose of this exercise?

Covey did this because you should be doing now whatever it is you want to be remembered for doing or being. If you want to be remembered as generous after you are gone, then you need to give *now*. If you want to leave a legacy of purpose, you must be doing your purpose *now*. From there, Covey directs each reader to write a personal mission statement. I have had such a statement for many years and it helped me practice all the habits, but especially Habit Two. I want to be remembered as a writer, so guess what that means? I must write now, since I can't write when I'm dead.

PurposeCoach Tips

Helping people in your business to apply the Eight Habits (seven plus voice or purpose) is good business in the long run. It will help your employees be more productive and focused.

If you aren't a leader or manager in your current position, you still need to be a person of the Eight Habits. Perhaps you will find that you are in the wrong position in the right company or the wrong (or right) position in the wrong company.

Begin with the "End in Mind"—where do

you want to be in your work in five years? What steps can you take today to be there five years from now?

Purpose in the Family

Mr. Covey also wrote a book entitled, *The 7 Habits of Highly Effective Families*. In that book, the habits are the same but he applies them to a family setting. Covey has a list of hints for each habit to help families work through and master the seven habits. Here are few from the end of his chapter on "Begin with the End in Mind":

1. Set aside a time when each family member tells one strength he or she has noticed about a designated child. Write them down. Keep these in mind as you develop your family mission statement. Continue until everyone has had a turn.

2. Make a family flag, select a family motto, or write a family song.

I have mentioned three books by Stephen Covey, all of which I would recommend for your purpose studies. They are not "easy read" books, but books that will add a great deal to your understanding of who you are. I taught the *Seven-Habits* material years before I taught about purpose. It was instrumental in preparing me for what I'm doing today as well as in my becoming a highly effective person.

Personal Purpose

Are you discouraged or encouraged with your

PurposeQuest? I am still making progress on my own, and I have been on the journey for almost 40 years. In 2005, I made an adjustment to my purpose statement, changing it from *bringing* order out of chaos to *creating* order out of chaos. That was a big deal for me since I embraced my creativity and de-emphasized my administrative gifts for the first time in my adult life. Now I have made another change to my statement. (This is so interesting because I went 22 years without a change and now I had two changes in a short period of time.)

I now define my purpose as "creating order out of chaos *without control*." This acknowledges that I have always created order without any power or position of authority—I have created order as a servant leader. This is once again a powerful and significant change for me. I share this with you to encourage you to keep searching and questing. It will pay dividends in the long run.

Wherever you are in your purpose journey, don't give up the quest. Go to my website and dive into the many resources there to help you. If you have a special need or are "stuck" and can't move forward, write and let me know the problem. I will write back and prescribe a possible solution.

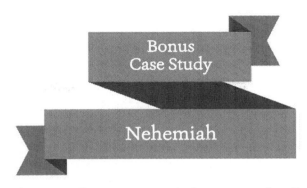

It's time for an extended case study focusing on the life of Nehemiah to garner some interesting and helpful purpose lessons from this man's life. (You may want to read the book of Nehemiah before you proceed.) In short, Nehemiah served the Persian king Artaxerxes, who ruled from 464-424 BC. In about 445 BC, Artaxerxes commissioned his servant Nehemiah to return and rebuild Jerusalem, the city of his fathers. This profile will study how Nehemiah got assigned to duty in Jerusalem and what he did once he arrived. We will see that Nehemiah was a man of purpose, otherwise he could not have done the great work he did.

Quality Questions Produce a Quality Life

The book of Nehemiah begins with Nehemiah asking the men who had come from Jerusalem some questions: "In the month of Kislev in the twentieth year, while I was in the citadel of Susa, Hanani, one of my brothers, came from Judah with some other men, and I questioned them about the Jewish remnant that survived the exile, and also about Jerusalem" (Nehemiah 1:1-2).

Most people don't know their purpose

because they don't ask enough questions. I heard a motivational speaker say once that quality questions lead to a quality life. What he meant was that you must seek the truth concerning who you are, and part of that seeking is asking the right questions—and waiting for and pursuing the answers.

Nehemiah was interested in Jerusalem and its residents, even though he had never been there. This group of travelers piqued his interest and he asked a lot of questions. Their answers provoked him to prayer, thought, and action. The rest is history.

When I first found my purpose, it was because I asked God, "If you didn't create me to start this business that failed, what *did* You create me to do?" That was a quality question. Through a series of events, I concluded the answer was, "You are here to create order out of chaos." That was a quality answer, the pursuit of which has led me to a quality life, one that enables me to do what I love all over the world. What questions are you currently asking? If quality questions lead to a quality life, do no questions lead to a nothing life?

What Makes You Cry?

What was Nehemiah's response to the answers to his questions? "When I heard these things, I sat down and wept. For some days I mourned and fasted and prayed before the God of heaven" (Nehemiah 1:4-5). I often substitute the word passion for purpose. Passion is a driving force that activates your creativity and will to do something. Tears of joy and sorrow often accompany your passion as you respond and make yourself vulnerable and available to a need that exists in the world. The first time I spoke about purpose, people in the room wept. I have seen thousands more cry over the years. Tears and purpose seem to go together hand-in-hand.

In 1998, I was watching a television documentary about the suffering of women in Afghanistan. I remember praying, "Lord, why am I crying? If you need someone to go to Afghanistan, I'm willing." In 2003, I received an invitation to go to Afghanistan from people I didn't even know. I went and it changed my life and the course of my ministry.

What makes you cry? I'm not talking only about tears of sorrow. Can you sit and listen to some kind of music and cry? Do you cry during a sad movie? Cry with joy when someone is blessed? If you do, then go back to the first point and ask the Lord, "Why am I crying?" The answers may surprise you and hold clues to help you clarify your purpose. It certainly did for Nehemiah.

"Well, I Sort Of, Like, You Know…"

Nehemiah prayed and fasted to clarify his passion and the way forward. Then his big break came. One day he was serving the king and the king noticed that Nehemiah was sad. Let's read the rest in Nehemiah's own words:

> The king said to me, "What is it you want?"
> Then I prayed to the God of heaven, and I
> answered the king, "If it pleases the king and
> if your servant has found favor in his sight,

let him send me to the city in Judah where my fathers are buried so that I can rebuild it." Then the king, with the queen sitting beside him, asked me, "How long will your journey take, and when will you get back?" It pleased the king to send me; so I set a time. I also said to him, "If it pleases the king, may I have letters to the governors of Trans-Euphrates, so that they will provide me safe-conduct until I arrive in Judah? And may I have a letter to Asaph, keeper of the king's forest, so he will give me timber to make beams for the gates of the citadel by the temple and for the city wall and for the residence I will occupy?" And because the gracious hand of my God was upon me, the king granted my requests. So I went to the governors of Trans-Euphrates and gave them the king's letters. The king had also sent army officers and cavalry with me (Nehemiah 2:4-9).

You must be able to state your purpose and goals with clarity and conviction. When the king asked Nehemiah what he wanted, Nehemiah had a ready answer. The king clearly understood what Nehemiah wanted and could then either say yes or no.

At times, I will ask people what they think their purpose is. It's then that I see how difficult it is for some people to talk about themselves. They will often say something like this: "Well, I think my purpose is, sort of, like, to help people. Yeah, that's it. And I probably, you know, encourage other people, but of course, it's not me, it's the Lord."

Does that sound like clarity? You can't state your purpose while prefacing it with phrases like "I think," "probably," or "maybe." You either know your purpose or you don't. What's more, if you can't overcome the natural or learned hesitancy many have talking about themselves, you will always struggle to come up with a clear statement.

Let's Review

In this study, we learned three purpose lessons from Nehemiah's profile.

1. You may not know your purpose because you don't ask enough questions

2. Tears often go hand in hand with purpose, so what makes you cry?

3. You must be able to state your purpose and goals with clarity and conviction.

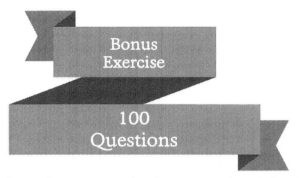

Bonus
Exercise

100
Questions

If good questions lead to a quality life, then is stands to reason that 100 questions would lead to a fantastic life. There is a recommended exercise in a book by Michael Gelb entitled *How to Think Like Leonardo da Vinci.* Here is a recommendation that Gelb made:

> In your notebook, make a list of a hundred questions that are important to you. Your list can include any kind of question as long as it's something you deem significant: anything from "How can I save more money?" or "how can I have more fun?" to "What is the meaning and purpose of my existence?" and "How can I best serve the Creator?"

> Do the entire list in one sitting. Write quickly; don't worry about spelling, grammar, or repeating the same question in different words (recurring questions will alert you to emerging themes). Why a hundred questions? The first twenty or so will be "off the top of your head." In the next thirty or forty themes often begin to emerge. And, in the latter part of the

second half of the list you are likely to discover unexpected but profound material.

When you have finished, read through your list and highlight the themes that emerge. Consider the emerging themes without judging them. Are most of your questions about relationships? Business? Fun? Money? The meaning of life?[9]

I recently produced my hundred questions in about 30 minutes. It was a valuable exercise that I will be processing for quite some time. I took the exercise one step further and went to a place that has some additional ready-made questions for you and I to ponder.

More Good Questions

Where did I go? I went to the Bible, specifically the gospels in the New Testament. At one time, I noticed how often Jesus asked questions when He taught and preached, so I decided to pull those questions out and put them in one document. I found about 150 questions (there are more, but some are duplicates or closely resemble other questions). Some of the questions Jesus asked were, "What do you want me to do for you?" or "Why do you doubt?" or "Why are you afraid?"

After identifying those questions in the gospels, I wondered if I could turn Jesus' questions into a daily devotional, even though I did not have enough for 366 days. I expanded my search for questions to include the epistles, the psalms and proverbs, and other books of the Bible. When I went looking, I found more than enough and produced *What Would Jesus Ask You Today? 366 Challenging Questions from God's Word*.

Posing questions to ourselves should be a way of life. We should be searching for both questions and answers that will help us grow and stimulate new ways of thinking. Why is this important? It's important because of what Paul wrote in Romans 12:1-2:

> Therefore, I urge you, brothers and sisters, in view of God's mercy, to offer your bodies as a living sacrifice, holy and pleasing to God— this is your true and proper worship. Do not conform to the pattern of this world, but be transformed by the renewing of your mind. Then you will be able to test and approve what God's will is—his good, pleasing and perfect will.

If we think differently, then we will be transformed because our minds are being renewed. It's essential that we all change the way we think if we are going to find and fulfill purpose, for a new purpose chapter in your life cannot be written with your old life story. We need a new narrative and that's where the 100-question exercise and the questions from Scripture come into play.

Gathering the questions can be a challenge, but getting the answers can be even more difficult. If you are going to be a person of purpose, however, you must do the work and spend the time pursuing the direction and insight these questions can bring.

Your Assignment

Your assignment is clear: Sit down and write out your own list of 100 questions. Then supplement your list with the list of questions you can locate from the Bible. Does this seem like a lot of work? It may be, but let me ask you a question (another good question coming up): Is this work worth it if you can clarify your purpose? In your pursuit of a quality life, make your quality question list and study it. See what patterns emerge as you follow in the steps of Nehemiah by asking quality questions.

CHAPTER 5
Purpose is Practical

Years ago, I was in Oklahoma City conducting my purpose seminar when a woman approached me after the class. She noticed I was living in Mobile, Alabama and was connected to Mobile through an association with the Junior Miss Society as their state director. She asked if I would be willing to come and speak to her colleagues at the Junior Miss Association.

Over the years, I have had many people come forward to ask me a similar question, and only a few follow up on the inquiry. This woman in Oklahoma City did, however, and several months later I found myself speaking at a retreat attended by every state director and the Junior Miss board of directors. (The Junior Miss was a national program providing scholarship opportunities for young women graduating from high school. They have since changed their name to Distinguished Young Women.)

Since you know my purpose, you know why I was there. Without me knowing it, the Society was experiencing chaos and I was there to bring order. I shared what I knew and found out later that my input helped turn the organization around. They invited me back to speak at their opening breakfast of their annual event and I had a chance to talk with 50 of the finest high school young ladies in the United States—and you know I talked to them about purpose!

My point is that my purpose has involved me with people and real-life situations and problems. In other words, the expression or fulfillment of my purpose is practical. It allows me to help people at all levels of life, sometimes spiritual and sometimes not.

Too often people I talk to about purpose consider purpose as something only for the famous or super-spiritual. Or they often are content to define purpose in hard-to-understand terms that have no meaning for everyday life or are difficult to measure the results. For example, if someone says, "My purpose is to improve the quality of life and preserve planet earth to be enjoyed by future generations and love everyone and be kind to animals," the person has stated some things that are general and defy explanation of how they will be accomplished. The example is a good values statement (I preserve the environment, I protect animals, I enhance quality of life for those around me), but they are not purpose statements until they become practical. How will you improve the quality of life? How have you already been doing that? How can you do it more effectively? Just saying it is not enough; you must find ways with God's help to do it.

As I write, my latest expression of creating order out of chaos is through my publishing company, Urban Press. I work mostly with first-time authors who will sometimes bring me a 10,000-word manuscript and think it is a 150-page book (in reality, they only have about 35 pages). I then work with them to draw more material from their life story and work. As we do that, we confront confusion, fear, distrust, anxiety, and more fear. All that represents chaos, and often I interview them and take their comments, transcribe them, and mold them into a book project. Can you see how practical my purpose is expressed through my publishing efforts?

I also do a lot of work in Kenya, East Africa, and have seen my purpose expressed there as well. I take many people on tours and have founded libraries, adopted orphans, and done relief work among the poor. No one guided me through how to do all that. I had to confront the chaos and create order to it so that needy children and people could be helped.

I hope you are getting the point. Your goal is not to craft a beautifully-worded purpose; your goal is to be a person of purpose who knows what your purpose is and is doing it. It is not enough for us to declare our purpose or wear a t-shirt with a slogan on it. If my purpose is to create order, then I must be busy doing that. I need to devote my available time to finding the chaos and creating the order. I need to become more skilled at recognizing chaos while confronting my own fears and feelings of inadequacy so I am not content to talk about what I can do, but *doing* it.

Years ago, I had the privilege of baptizing a Chinese student who was in the United States. This man had decided to become a follower of Jesus and for him that meant entering the baptismal waters. As he stood waist deep in the pool, he asked for his Chinese Bible and turned to John 3:16. He read in Chinese and translated for us in English. When he did, he put a new twist into a familiar passage when he read, "For God so loved people that He gave. . ." Now that is not accurate to the original Greek translation, but it is still true. God loves people.

He loves them so much that He made you and me. When He made us, He gave us a purpose, some part of Himself or an assignment so important to Him that when people touch us, they are touching part of Him. You have heard it said you are God's hands and feet on earth and therefore it's up to you to carry out His plan through your purpose. I am God's agent to help people publish their stories. When I sit with people and guide them through the process, I am serving as their pastor at that moment. I am guiding them through an intimidating journey that seems chaotic to them, but is clear to me—because God helps me do it.

If you are a good listener, so is God. If you can extract the precious from the worthless, so does God. Your ability to function in your purpose through the power of God is proof of God's love, not just for you, but for the people around you. I can create order out of chaos because that is a part of who God is: "God is not a God of disorder, but of peace" (1 Corinthians 14:33). When I function in my purpose, I am expressing one aspect of God's love and care to the world around me. That care expresses itself in practical ways to some people or organizations I didn't even know God was interested in—like the Junior Miss. He is interested because that's where people live and God loves people. Consider one aspect of this truth from the Old Testament:

> Then the Lord said to Moses, "See, I have chosen Bezalel son of Uri, the son of Hur, of the tribe of Judah, and I have filled him with the Spirit of God, with skill, ability and knowledge in all kinds of crafts–to make artistic designs for work in gold, silver and bronze, to cut and set stones, to work in wood, and to engage in all kinds of craftsmanship. Moreover, I have appointed Oholiah son of Ahismach, of the tribe of Dan, to help him" (Exodus 31:1-6).

Bezalel was "filled with the Spirit of God" not to preach, do church work, sing songs, or write books. He was filled with God's Spirit to work with his hands. He had a practical craft that was spiritual from the start, for we behold God's handiwork when we look at His creation. Bezalel could have dismissed this as insignificant or a talent he had or training he had received from his father. God saw his skill from a different perspective, however, and that meant Bezalel needed to learn to see it that way too.

First and foremost, Bezalel's purpose was to serve

God's purpose, but his purpose was practical. He brought beauty out of raw materials. This beauty drew people's attention to God and His creation and led people to worship in the tabernacle God designed but Bezalel helped build. God is not removed from the everyday affairs of men and women. He has created you and wants you to be His agent in your part of the world as you function in your purpose. Maybe God wants you to bring beauty into the lives of others through music, dance, or some other creative expression. Whatever it is, it is practical and will touch people where they live.

Bezalel had a helper whose name was Oholiab. Oholiab wasn't just hired help or his assistant. He was appointed by God to assist the main man. His "help" wasn't an occupation, it was his life's purpose. God was with him and showed him how to be a good helper, because God comes alongside us and helps us do what He created us to do by giving us gifts, wisdom, and experience. Oholiab was simply expressing an aspect of God's personality to the world around him while he served God and Bezalel in a metal shop.

When Adam was created, God told him to "be fruitful and increase in number; fill the earth and subdue it" (Genesis 1:28). That was completely practical. Adam was to work at having a family and at subduing the earth. His purpose was to "rule over the fish of the sea and the birds of the air and over every living creature that moves on the ground" (Genesis 1:29). That did not involve church work.

I am not minimizing church work but it is

important to understand it is not the only or most important way to serve God. The most important way is for you to find and fulfill your God-given purpose. If you were born to fulfill your purpose through church work, then do it with all the strength God provides. If you weren't, stop trying to be what you are not. Maybe you were born for business, art, movies, or technology. Maybe God wants to send you to Babylon like He sent Daniel to express your purpose (and God's love) for a foreign culture and people.

If you try to be something God never intended you to be, then you are trying to improve on who and what God has made you, and that's a mistake. If you are good enough for God, why would you try to go against the counsel of His will and be something *you* think would honor Him? Be yourself and allow God to invest you in whatever way He chooses according to the purpose He has given you, all the while looking to improve and excel. As you develop, you must look for ways to be practical.

Remember, God loves the world and the people in it. He created you to be a gift to the world (and people) as you express your individual purpose in some practical way. If you are good enough for God, don't try to imitate someone else who is functioning successfully in their purpose and think you are pleasing God. Be yourself and go with the flow. In the end, you'll be content as you feel God's pleasure helping you be who He made you to be.

When I conduct leadership development seminars, I ask those present to come to a conclusion based on these three questions:

1. Is failure a learning experience?
2. Do you often learn more from failure than success?
3. Are you always to be learning and growing as a leader?

Everyone usually answers yes to those three questions, and then I pop the big one: 4. Therefore, shouldn't you be failing as often as possible?

At this point, people either stay quiet or answer no, so I go back over the first three questions. I am trying to get them to be comfortable with failure, which is inevitable. The fear of failure keeps many people from attempting to do what they are capable of doing, thus never discovering or developing their potential.

After doing this for years, I made an important adjustment recently to the final question. I now ask, "Therefore, shouldn't you be failing *on purpose* as often as possible?" I added those two words because all failure is not a learning experience. Being married five times or declaring bankruptcy three times is not the kind of failure I wanted people to embrace. My goal was for them to embrace purpose and not be afraid to fail and learn as they pursued something important.

I have written 38 books as of this updated version

of *I Wrote This Book on Purpose*. None of them are best-sellers; some have sold a few copies. I have failed, if my goal is to sell books, but I have learned from each book. Now, I have overcome my fears and I am writing fiction that includes teaching lessons in the stories. I have yet to achieve my sales goals—perhaps I never will—but I am failing on purpose, doing something I love and feel called to do. Perhaps my books will sell after I'm gone or maybe they will never sell. My point is that I am failing and learning, and it has made me a better coach and writer. Now I am publishing other people's work and my writing is my pedigree to help them write and create.

Where are you avoiding the pain of failure, thus forfeiting the growth you need to be a person of purpose? Now, let's get busy with this PurposeCoach session.

Purpose in the Church

The Old Testament prophet Samuel is an interesting study in purpose. His mother, Hannah, was in agony because she could not conceive. She dedicated her son to the Lord *before* he was born, God healed her, and then she gave birth to a son. After his birth, she made good on her promise and brought her little boy to the house of the Lord at Shiloh to serve and be tutored by the priest Eli. You can read this story for yourself in 1 Samuel 1-3.

When Samuel was serving in the house of the Lord, God called and spoke to him. Even though he was young, God gave Samuel a "hard word" concerning Eli, the ruling priest, and his family. We learn from the story that Eli's sons were useless in God's service, but Eli never confronted them. He refused to deal with his sons' issues, so God promised He would deal with the problem by removing them all from the priestly office. Here are a few things to consider about this situation:

1. Samuel came to serve in the Lord's house, but God set the agenda for Samuel's life. God raised up Samuel as a prophet and not a priest and expected Eli to cooperate with His plan.

2. God spoke to Samuel at an early age about His plan, which was Samuel's purpose.

3. When Samuel gave Eli the hard word that his family was in trouble, Eli could have seen Samuel as the problem as Saul did with David. Eli did not seek revenge, however, nor did not try to hinder Samuel in any way.

4. All Israel began to recognize Samuel as a prophet because "the Lord let none of his [Samuel's] words fall to the ground."

5. Samuel did not have to go looking for his purpose; his purpose came looking for him.

6. Samuel was not afraid, but approached the Lord with childlike faith and trust, and was given an important life assignment.

What can learn from these five points about purpose and the modern church. Here is what I see from the five points listed above.

1. We need to give people opportunities to serve in the Church, but always with a view toward finding out what God wants them to do. Don't put someone in the nursery and hold them there so the nursery work can get done. Stay close to that person and see what God is saying and doing in his or her life so they can be placed where they are most effective according to their gifts and purpose.

2. Workers, members, and followers must not allow leadership to usurp God's role in defining purpose. Eli didn't appoint Samuel as a prophet; only God could do that. Eli's role was to urge Samuel to respond to God when Samuel heard God's voice. The Church needs to teach people to hear God's voice and then to know what to do with what they have heard.

3. The church needs to raise up new leadership that God ordains. Leadership training and development are important tasks for every church, and purpose awareness is a critical part of someone's leadership development. It is not wrong for family to follow family in ministry, but it must be according to the will of God, otherwise nepotism creeps into the church. When that happens, the church's work is hindered.

4. Samuel had a public role and people began to recognize what he did with the help of God's anointing. We need to expose people to their life's work in the church and allow them to shine and gain a "following."

5. Purpose allows Paul's words to be fulfilled:

The eye cannot say to the hand, "I don't need you!" And the head cannot say to the feet, "I don't need you!" On the contrary, those parts of the body that seem to be weaker are indispensable, and the parts that we think are less honorable we treat with special honor. And the parts that are unpresentable are treated with special modesty, while our presentable parts need no special treatment. But God has combined the members of the body and has given greater honor to the parts that lacked it, so that there should be no division in the body, but that its parts should have equal concern for each other. If one part suffers, every part suffers with it; if one part is honored, every part rejoices with it Now you are the body of Christ, and each one of you is a part of it. And in the church God has appointed first of all apostles, second prophets, third teachers, then workers of miracles, also those having gifts of healing, those able to help others, those with gifts of administration, and those speaking in different kinds of tongues. Are all apostles? Are all prophets? Are all teachers? Do all work miracles? Do all have gifts of healing? Do all speak in tongues? Do all interpret? But eagerly desire the greater gifts (1 Corinthians 12:21-31).

Gifts and purpose cannot be obtained by going to a seminar or by preaching to someone. They only come through the work of the Holy Spirit. Church leaders need to help people find and fulfill their God-given purpose.

PurposeCoach Tips

Each person has a responsibility to hear God's voice to know his or her purpose. Then each person must function in that purpose whenever possible.

If a church is to grow and prosper, that church must systematically work to help people hear what God is saying to them, report it to leadership when possible, and then have leadership work to equip and release these people to their life's work—whether it is in or outside the church walls.

If leadership isn't doing or can't do this, then it is the responsibility of each person to do it as best they can with God's help, just as Samuel did. You can reference my book *Changing the Way*

We Do Church: 7 Steps to a Purposeful Reformation to learn more about what the church can do to train and release people of purpose.

CASE STUDY: Read 1 Samuel 1-3 and answer the following questions:

1. Does it surprise you that God spoke to young Samuel and gave him such a hard word?

2. As a leader, what are you doing to know and then cooperate with the word of the Lord in other's lives?

3. What are you doing as a leader to give people public opportunities to shine and express purpose? As a follower, what you are doing to help this happen? Remember, God doesn't promote potential but people who have honed their potential.

4. Has God spoken to you, but you are mistaking the voice for someone or something else? Try what Samuel did when you think a recurring thought of something you need to do or be it. Say, "Speak, Lord, for your servant listens.

Purpose in the Marketplace

I was in Malawi doing some consulting work for a bank. We were doing some team-building exercises. All the top leadership was there, including the bank's chief financial officer (CFO). During our time together, I noticed some bank promotions that I considered quite well done. When I commented on that, the CFO smiled and said, "I came up with that."

I was surprised he did, and it led to a discussion of

his role and life's work of being an accountant. To make a long story short, the CFO made a decision that day to apply for the chief marketing officer position in his bank. He could have been content to serve out his days with the bank in his accountant's role because that was what he had always done. The bank could have refused to consider the change, but both the CFO and the bank were more interested in results than propriety.

Many companies, both profit and nonprofit, don't see it as important to help people find where they are most productive. They hire, put people in place, and evaluate what kind of job they are doing. They expect results and, if the results aren't there, then they take remedial action that can eventually lead to termination. They miss the point that pursuing individual purpose is good business, for it places the people where they have the best chance for success and ongoing productivity and creativity.

PurposeCoach Tips

Talk to your human resources department about a plan to identify what people do best. Go back and use the questions in PurposeCoach session three to help understand what motivates your team members.

Consider bringing in a consultant to do some team-building work with your team that includes personality assessments and follow-up interviews. Often people will give information to an outsider that they won't divulge to someone in the company about what they love or dislike about their work.

CASE STUDY: Read Genesis 40:1-5, 20-23; 41:1-4, 33-57; 47:1-4. In this study, you will learn lessons from the life of Joseph's Pharaoh about helping people who are working for you to find and fulfill their purpose—and see how that practice is good for business.

Egypt in Joseph's times was the most powerful nation in the world. When Joseph first arrived, Egypt prospered under Pharaoh's leadership and there was no end in sight. While Joseph was imprisoned, the drama played out that led to Pharaoh's famous doubleheader dreams. Joseph helped Pharaoh understand the dreams and what the nation needed to do to prepare. The period leading up to the dream, the dream interpretation, and the dream application all give us valuable lessons from Pharaoh's leadership that we would do well to emulate.

Pharaoh's Leadership Lessons

What can we learn about Pharaoh from these passages?

1. **Pharaoh made quick decisions when he found the right person.** There was no procrastination when Pharaoh decided to act. Pharaoh knew he had found a "star" in Joseph and he acted quickly to secure his services and wisdom. Joseph was young

and had a shady past, but had wisdom. Good people are hard to find and sometimes harder to manage. When you find them, hire them!

2. **Pharaoh partnered with his opposite.** Pharaoh didn't fill his staff with people like him. Instead, he brought in some "opposites." Pharaoh hired a good operations man in Joseph to carry out the day-to-day plans of the kingdom. Partnering with your opposite can be difficult, for they see reality and life in contrast to your viewpoint. They can, however, see what you can't (and vice versa), thus strengthening the team through diversity and friendly dissent.

3. **Pharaoh recognized the importance of talent, gifting, and "special ability."** When Pharaoh met Joseph's brothers, he made an interesting comment: "If any of them have special ability, put them over my own flocks" (Genesis 47:6). He didn't give Joseph's brothers a job because they needed one or because they were Joseph's brothers. Don't hire *anyone* simply because they need a job or are related to you or someone already on staff.

4. **Pharaoh gave authority and established boundaries.** Pharaoh put Joseph in charge of operations to store food for the famine and then to distribute food in the famine.

Joseph's job description and expectations were clear; there was no ambiguity. While Joseph's hiring was a quick one, his job description was concise and well thought out.

5. **Pharaoh used his power to empower the right people**. All leaders have power. What distinguishes a great from a good or bad leader is how that power is used. Pharaoh used his power to empower Joseph to do the job that God had gifted him to do. Pharaoh used his power correctly; he used it to help his team get the job done. He listened to Joseph's strategy and then approved it. With his stamp of approval, he then let Joseph do it with a minimum of input or interference.

Conclusions

Pharaoh was rewarded well for his exceptional leadership skills. His country was saved from oblivion and suffering. Pharaoh secured a place in history as a good leader, in contrast to his counterpart who wielded heavy-handed, authoritarian control during the time of Moses.

What kind of leader do you want to be? I hope you want to be one like Joseph's Pharaoh. Take some time to reflect on your style as it relates to Pharaoh's and see where you need to improve to help your organization benefit from your team's pursuit of individual purpose. Then set about building a more effective team than you have now so you and your organization can be the fullest, best expression of who it is God intended you to be.

Purpose in the Family

Let's return to our study of Samuel, which we began earlier in this session. This time, however, let's study the issue of purpose from a family perspective. Re-read 1 Samuel 1-3, focusing on the role Hannah had in her son's purpose.

Here are some points I see and questions (quality questions, I might add) to ask yourself. Feel free to add your insight and questions to the list:

1. Samuel's purpose was borne out of Hannah's suffering from being childless. Is there a role that your sufferings or sacrifices have played or will play in your children's purpose? This pertains to nieces and nephews as well.

2. Hannah made commitments concerning her son *before* he was born. What role are you playing in shaping your child's purpose? Too often, parents want to be popular with their children instead of serving as their mentors and coaches for purpose and productivity. Or, parents want their children to fulfill society's expectations so they direct their children to think career and financial security instead of purpose.

3. Hannah turned Samuel over to Eli when he was a young boy. After that, she only saw her son once a year. I am not implying

you must send your child away early in life, but there are important principles to see from her example. Have you released your child(ren) to God's plan? Are you co-operating with that plan? Are you looking for your child(ren) to fulfill some need in your life they were never intended to fill?

4. Hannah had other children, but we don't know who they were or what they did. Every child is different and must be taught to follow his or her own path to purpose. Remember the proverb, "Train a child in the way he should go, and when he is old he will not turn from it" (Proverbs 22:6). God will give you wisdom to see the way your child should go—but it's not your way, it's God's way for them.

It is of note that Hannah's boy is still speaking to the church today because Hannah did her job. You won't have those results with most of your children, if any, but that doesn't prevent or preclude you from playing the role only a parent, grandparent, aunt, or uncle can play in the purposeful development of young family members.

PurposeCoach Tips

Try not to talk to your children only about what they can do to make a living. I have

counseled many frustrated adults who abandoned their dream or purpose because their parents or other family members told them to be more "responsible." Your objective is to make your family more purposeful, not more responsible.

This does not mean you should not help your child(ren) find a career. Don't advise them to be accountants, however, because "accountants can always find work," if they hate numbers or dislike being tied down to one place (like a desk) for long periods of time. For example, if your child loves sports and wants to play in the NBA, nurture their dream, but then expand their world to understand that they can be in the NBA as a coach, trainer, agent, broadcaster, scout, or statistician, or by working for a team in the front office.

Personal Purpose

As stated earlier, the main reason why more people don't know their purpose is that they don't ask or keep on asking until they find an answer. God is a great communicator and wants you to know your purpose more than you do. I no longer put my faith in my ability to hear the Lord; I put my trust in God's ability to speak to me. Here is where Proverbs 2:1-8 is so helpful:

> My son, if you *accept* my words and *store up my commands* within you, *turning your ear* to wisdom and *applying your heart* to understanding, and *if you*

call out for insight and *cry aloud* for understanding, and *if* you *look for it* as for silver and *search for it* as for hidden treasure, then *you will understand* the fear of the Lord and *find* the knowledge of God. For the Lord gives wisdom, and from his mouth come knowledge and understanding. He holds victory in store for the upright, he is a shield to those whose walk is blameless, for he guards the course of the just and protects the way of his faithful ones (emphasis added)

Notice all the words and phrases in italics in those eight verses. There is nothing passive about any of them. They point to the need to be relentless in your search for life's wisdom, which would include knowing your purpose. With that in mind, let's review the basic questions I ask anyone who is on their PurposeQuest.

1. For what have people complimented you on a regular basis?

2. What gives you joy and excites your will?

3. How would you spend your time if money to live on wasn't an issue?

4. What did you find yourself daydreaming about when you were child, or even as an adult?

5. What makes you angry? What makes you cry?

6. What do you do that when you do it, you lose track of time and forget to eat?

7. Is there a Bible verse or passage that

accurately explains who you are or what you do best?

8. What are you afraid of that is keeping you from embracing your purpose?

9. Has a godly person spoken anything to you that described who you are or what you would do?

10. If you lost your job tomorrow and had a six-month severance package, what would you do during those six months?

Keeping in mind the advice from Proverbs 2, seek and keep on seeking the answers. Write down your thoughts for every question and talk about them with your family, friends, mentors, or spiritual advisers. Don't give up seeking and you will surely find the answers.

I hope you are encouraged right now in your PurposeQuest. If you need more help, go to my website and utilize the many resources that are there to assist you. If you have a specific need or are "stuck" and can't move forward, write and let me know the problem. I will write back and suggest a possible solution.

CHAPTER 6
Purpose Brings Pleasure

In my younger days, I loved planning conferences and special events. When I witnessed people arriving to an event I had planned, I always got a rush of joy that was hard to describe. I didn't even have to sit in the sessions or listen to the speakers to appreciate the conference. Seeing the results of my work when people came and enjoyed themselves was good enough for me. As soon as the event was over, no matter how hard I had worked or how well it had gone (or not gone), I was always ready to plan another one.

There is no way to explain this joyful feeling apart from my purpose. My purpose is to create order out of chaos. I loved taking a concept for a meeting, talking it through so everyone understood what the "end result" should look like, and then creating something (a program, the budget, facilities, brochure, and finally, the event) out of an idea. My purpose was not to organize conferences; my purpose of creating order out of chaos was expressed in that role, and it brought me great joy for many years.

The concept of joy in fulfilling your purpose can be a tricky one. For many, pleasure or happiness is not a good indicator of what anyone was born to do. Some feel that pleasure is too easily sidetracked into selfish pursuits often in opposition to the will of God. Others don't trust their happiness barometer. If it feels good, it can't *be* good no matter how good or righteous it seems to be. For some, joy shouldn't be a motivating factor, and if it's present, it's really a bonus. (I know I used joy, happiness, and pleasure interchangeably in this paragraph. I will explain later.)

At one seminar I was conducting, I had a pianist tell me, "I loved playing the piano so much that I gave it up." I was incredulous and found out that this person was currently doing something she tolerated rather than pursue the activity she loved. She was so afraid her piano skills could become an idol that she decided to abandon them altogether. Rather than take that risk of messing up what she loved doing, she gave it up to pursue a job that paid her some money—and at which, by her own admission, she was miserable. What kind of God would give her a love for playing the piano and then ask her to walk away from it for the rest of her life? That is a concept I will never embrace, but I do understand the origins of her thinking.

I urged her to re-engage her piano playing but then to establish a board of directors (yes, a personal board of directors) to help her build boundaries in her life so she would not fall into the trap she described. They needed to be people who understood purpose and would protect her from overexertion but also from being over-cautious. I explained that purpose is consuming *because* it brings so much pleasure. When we read the Apostle Paul's description of what he did and what he endured to do what he did, we get the picture that purpose took over his life and he loved what he was doing. Otherwise, he could not have endured the hardships he did to fulfill his purpose.

In every one of my original seminars, I refer to the movie *Chariots of Fire*. In that movie, the missionary statesman Eric Liddell was preparing to run in the 1924 Olympics representing England. His sister confronted him in the movie, concerned that his training and running were taking him away from his missionary activities. The movie character responded with words the real-life Eric Liddell never said (but I wish he had): "But God made me fast, and when I run, I feel His pleasure!"

Joy is an indicator of what it is God made us to do and be. Man has abused the concept of pleasure but it is nevertheless an emotion God built into man's being. When used properly and under God's direction, pleasure or joy will direct us into God's will. If you have joy when you work with children, then you know God's will for your life. You don't have to pray or agonize, asking, "God, is it your will for me to work with children?"

You already have your answer. Our pleasure meter, so to speak, will register high readings when we serve the Lord by entering into His joy. There are legitimate joys to be savored that are not related to purpose, things like family, accomplishment, beauty, and the like. Those pleasures cannot compare, however, to the joy of *doing* what it is you were created to do and *knowing* it is what you were created to do.

Earlier, I used the terms pleasure, joy, and happiness interchangeably. I know some will object, pointing out that happiness and pleasure are tied to circumstances while joy may transcend circumstances. I would not disagree, but at the same time, effort to determine if you are happy or joyful is wasted energy. I was happy when I was planning conferences even when things went wrong. When did that happiness become joy? I don't know. I do know I volunteered for the next conference even after my greatest failures.

The issue when we look at joy or happiness is: Can happiness be a state of mind and can joy be related to activities we pursue? My answer is yes to both, so therefore I am not concerned about whether you are happy or joyful. Purpose brings pleasure, joy, and happiness, so I am not going to split hairs over which is which and what activates each.

John Piper, in his book *Desiring God: Meditations of a Christian Hedonist*, writes:

> Christian Hedonism is a philosophy of life built on the following five convictions:
> 1. The longing to be happy is a universal

human experience, and it is good, not sinful.

2. We should never try to deny or resist our longing to be happy, as though it was a bad impulse. Instead we should seek to intensify this longing and nourish it with whatever will provide the deepest and most enduring satisfaction.

3. The deepest and most enduring happiness is found only in God. Not from God, but in God.

4. The happiness we find in God reaches its consummation when it is shared with others in the manifold ways of love.

5. To the extent we try to abandon the pursuit of our own pleasure, we fail to honor God and love people. Or, to put it positively: the pursuit of pleasure is a necessary part of all worship and virtue. That is, the chief end of man is to glorify God by enjoying him forever.[10]

The reason I don't always distinguish between joy, pleasure, and happiness is that it creates a fear in someone's mind that they have pleasure, but is it God's will? I tell those people to trust God and follow their hearts, believing the enjoyment or pleasure or whatever they call it is God's will. Therefore, they can move toward it in faith. It makes life a lot simpler.

Solomon wrote, "So I saw that there is nothing better for a man than to enjoy his work, because that is his lot" (Ecclesiastes 3:22) and "Then I realized that it is good and proper for a man to eat and drink, and to find satisfaction in his toilsome labor under the sun during the few days of life God has given him—for this is his lot" (Ecclesiastes 5:18). If Solomon summarized his life-long pursuit of wisdom with those statements, don't you think what you enjoy doing is at least some indication of what your life's purpose is?

Laurence Boldt shares a story in his previously mentioned book, *How to Find the Work You Love*:

> When Mother Teresa was going through a period of self-questioning and doubt prior to finding her own life's work, she sought the advice of a wise man. She asked him how she would know if she had found her true calling in life. The advice he gave in reply is something we all do well to remember. As he told her, you will know you have found your work "if you are happy. . . . Profound joy of heart is like a magnet that indicates the path of life. One has to follow it even though one enters into a way full of difficulties."
>
> That is what is meant by finding a life's work, by doing the work you love. It is not necessarily that it is always easy or even always pleasurable. On the contrary, true love has the element of sacrifice, a readiness to suffer for something greater than oneself. Yet, as Samuel Johnson put it, "He that labors in any great or laudable undertaking has his fatigues first

supported by hope, and afterwards rewarded by joy."[11]

What do you do that when you do it, you feel peaceful and maybe even exhilarated? What do you dream about doing that if you did do it, you would be happy? Is it travel? Starting a business? A ministry? Giving away large (or small) sums of money? Singing before a large audience? Writing a book? Whatever it is, don't ignore it because you're afraid of the joy it might bring. Use the joy as an indicator that what you are considering doing is bringing joy because it is God's will for you. That joy can be a regular friend, not an occasional visitor, if you will engage your purpose more often.

As Boldt wrote, "It is not necessarily that it is always easy or even always pleasurable." To this we turn our attention in the next chapter, but only after another PurposeCoach session.

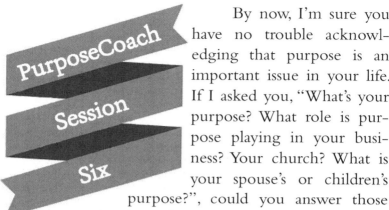

PurposeCoach Session Six

By now, I'm sure you have no trouble acknowledging that purpose is an important issue in your life. If I asked you, "What's your purpose? What role is purpose playing in your business? Your church? What is your spouse's or children's purpose?", could you answer those questions? I hope so, but if not, your PurposeCoach is here to help.

Here is an email I received from someone recently:

> My friend asked me to say thank you to you. I spoke to him on the phone yesterday. A couple of years ago you encouraged him to stay true to his heart for the urban areas.
>
> God just opened the door for him to become the director of a ministry in San Francisco that does just that. It is a dream job for him. He told me that it was like he was born to do this job. He is also going to be blessed financially through this position. He so appreciated your counsel and input; it helped him to stick with his heart.
>
> He wondered if the Lord had put him on the shelf. It was a three-year journey to find this ministry, or for it to find him. :-) John, thanks

for doing what God has called you to do. You are making a difference!

I have many such stories that have come in from around the world, and I am anxious to add your story to the mix. Without further ado, let's move into the next-to-last coaching session in this book.

Purpose in the Church

Everywhere I go, I hear people quoting Philippians 4:13 in regards to purpose and productivity. People tell me "I can do all things through Christ who strengthens me." I hate to be the bearer of bad news, but that's not true and that interpretation can be an obstacle to prevent people from finding their purpose. Before you burn this book or toss it in the trash because that is your favorite life verse, let me explain.

First, the context of any verse is important to understand and interpret it. The context for Philippians 4:13 is a financial and not a purpose context. Let's look at verse 12: "I know what it is to be in need, and I know what it is to have plenty. I have learned the secret of being content in any and every situation, whether well fed or hungry, whether living in plenty or in want. I can do everything through him who gives me strength."

We must stop assigning people projects and work in the church according to what needs to be done while paying no attention to what people have gifts or capacity to do. It doesn't produce good results. Too often we have not offered a variety of ministry work, but have instead asked people to "fit into" one of a few roles we have to offer: ushering, nursery, choir, or the like. Then they resort to the I-can-do-all-things mentality.

When I administer one of the many spiritual gifts profiles on the market today, I am fascinated to watch people process the results. Many look at their lowest scores and say, "Great. This lets me know what I need to work on." Now think about that comment. A gift is a gift. You either have it or you don't. How can you work on a gift that isn't there? You can't get gifted results from a person who isn't gifted in any area of work or ministry.

On every gifts profile I have taken, mercy comes up as my lowest score. When I was a pastor, I worked hard to come up with some mercy, often to no avail. Do you know what I did? I stopped trying. That's right, I crossed mercy off my to-do list. Instead, I began to focus on my strengths and gifts, which are teaching, administration, and leadership. I resigned from being what I call a Sunday pastor but did not quit church work. I have spent the last 30 years fashioning a world that enables me to write, teach, consult, and organize. I have been far more productive for God and less frustrated since I have done that.

You may object and demand to know, "What about mercy?" Well, I can't ignore mercy, that's true. Instead of working on it, I gave that area of my life to God for Him to produce mercy in me in the power of His Spirit. That process is referred to as the fruit of the Spirit in Galatians 5:22. The Spirit is producing mercy in me and I am a gentler, kinder administrator today—but it doesn't come naturally.

I know it's my weakness. I often rely on others

who have the mercy gift to help me understand what I should do and how I should act, but I don't spend any time trying to cultivate mercy. I will never, ever be a Mother Teresa, no matter how much I pray, work, or quote Philippians 4:13. Then again, she could never have been a John Stanko.

PurposeCoach Tips

Here is a suggestion for you to use in your small group, church staff, or family. Invest in one of the many spiritual gifts profiles available today (they are reasonably inexpensive). If you need any advice on which one to use, write me and we can look at the options. They don't take long to complete and would be valuable even if you have done them before.

When you get the results, don't let anyone focus on their lack. Direct their attention to their strengths and gifts and prayerful help them find ways to express who they are. Help them see how they can make their strengths stronger. Give them permission to be who they are and to stop trying to be who they're not. This may require that you lead a discussion about Philippians 4:13 and put the misconception to rest that someone can do anything if they have enough faith. That's not true where personality and giftedness are concerned. Deal with sin in your life but leave who God made you to be alone. It never produces good results when you try to improve on the handiwork He expressed when He created you and the people around you.

Purpose in the Marketplace

If you recall, we looked at a book by Marcus Buckingham in PurposeCoach session two. He wrote another book and I thought it would be helpful if I did a brief review for you, highlighting the main points he made. I want to do this because it fits in perfectly with what we discussed earlier, and flows with the general theme of PurposeCoach. Buckingham's book is entitled *The One Thing You Need to Know*. Here is the summary.

★ ★ ★ ★ ★

From all this, you can see the vital distinction between the role of the manager and that of the leader. Each is critically important to the sustained success of the organization, but the focus of each is entirely different.

The manager's starting point is the individual employee. He looks at her palette of talents, skills, knowledge, experience, and goals, and then uses these to design a specific future in which the individual can be successful. That person's success is his focus.

The leader sees things differently. He starts with his image of the future. This better future is what he talks about, thinks about, ruminates on, designs and refines. Only with this image clear in his mind does he turn his attention to persuading other people that they can be successful in the future he envisions. But through it all, the future remains his focus.

You can play both roles, of course, but if you do, you must know when to change gears. When you want to manage, begin with the person. When you want to lead, begin with the picture of where you are headed.

Exactly how you can play each of these roles most effectively is the subject of the next two chapters. Here we will discuss the skills you can learn and refine as you strive to make the best use of your natural talents for managing and leading.

★ ★ ★ ★ ★

THE MOST USEFUL QUESTIONS

"How can you identify these levers?"

Strengths and weakness, triggers, and unique style of learning—these are the three things you must know about a person in order to manage him effectively. But how can you identify them?

Well, obviously there's no substitution for observation. The great manager spends a good deal of time outside his office, walking around, watching each person's reactions, listening, taking mental notes about what each person is drawn to and what each person struggles with. Alison Fedeli, the manager of Wellington Hospital's twenty-seven person physiotherapy unit in London, describes the power of observation this way: "I think all the time people are telling you things. They're showing you who they are in small ways. The ones who don't want to sign in on time. The ones that don't finish their notes. The ones that are always there at the end of the day. The ones that…well, different things. People are telling you things all the time. And I think you've got to listen and watch out and observe that." So, yes, get out of your office and observe.

There's also value in having your employees take certain personality-type test such as StrengthsFinder, Myers-Briggs, Kolbe, or DISC. The results of these tests, although quite complex, can provide a structured framework and, most important, a common language for identifying how one person differs from another.

But, initially, the best way to identify these three levers is to ask a few simple questions and listen carefully to the answers. Of all the questions I've experimented with, these five have proven to be the most revealing.

For strengths:

1. What was the best day at work you've had in the last three months?

- What were you doing?
- Why did you enjoy it so much?

For weaknesses:

2. What was your worst day at work in the last three months?

- What were you doing?
- Why did it grate on you so much?

For triggers:

3. What was the best relationship with a manager you've ever had?

- What made it work so well?

4. What was the best praise or recognition you've ever received?

- What made it so good?

And for unique style of learning:

5. When in your career do you think you were learning the most?

- Why did you learn so much?
- What's the best way for you to learn?

I recommend asking these questions of each new hire. You can also ask them of each existing employee at the beginning of your financial year. This mini-interview will take only about half an hour, but it should be a rich half hour. Ask these five questions, listen closely, and then act on this information in the same way that Michelle, Judi, Russ, and Alison did, and you will see extraordinary results. You will discover the power of capitalizing on what is unique about each of your people.

★ ★ ★ ★ ★

We've delved into three multifaceted subjects—managing, leading, and sustained individual success—and have withstood, I hope, the temptation to land on one answer, one step, or one action that drives excellence. Instead we've found three controlling insights, three perspectives, that will serve you well as you strive to find success and satisfaction in this complex world of competing interests.

To excel as a manager you must never forget that each of your direct reports is unique and that your chief responsibility is not to eradicate this uniqueness, but rather to arrange roles, responsibilities, and expectations so that you can capitalize upon it. The more you perfect this skill, the more effectively you will turn talents into performance.

To excel as a leader requires the opposite skill. You must become adept at calling upon those needs we all share. Our common needs include the need for security, for community, for authority, and for respect, but, for you, the leader, the most powerful universal need is our need for clarity. To transform our fear of the unknown into confidence in the future, you must discipline yourself to describe our joint venture vividly and precisely. As your skill at this grows, so will our confidence in you.

And last, you must remember that your sustained success depends on your ability to cut out of your working life those activities, or people, that pull you off your strengths' path. Your leader can show you clearly your better future. Your manager can draft you on to the team and cast you into the right role on the team. However, it will always be *your* responsibility to make the small but significant course corrections that allow you to sustain your highest and best contribution to this team, and to the better future it is charged with creating. The more skilled you are at this, the more valued, and fulfilled, and successful you will become.

As we've seen in each of these roles, the critical skill is not balance, but its inverse, intentional imbalance. The great manager bets that he will prevail by magnifying, emphasizing, and then capitalizing on each employee's uniqueness. The great leader comes to a conclusion about his core customer, his organization's strength, its core score, and the actions he will commit to right now, and then, in the service of clarity, banishes from his thought and conversation almost everything else. The sustainably effective individual, by rigorously removing the irritants from his working life, engages with the world in an equally imbalanced fashion.

It takes insight to focus in this way, and discipline, and since lopsided bets can be scary, courage. My hope for this book is that it has served to strengthen in you all three.[12]

★ ★ ★ ★ ★

To learn more about *The One Thing You Need to Know*, please visit www.marcusbuckingham.com.

CASE STUDY: Take the five questions that Buckingham provided in the excerpt and ask them to your co-workers, spouse or anyone else with whom you have a working relationship.

PurposeCoach Tips

If you haven't already, take a personality-type profile online, through your work, or through PurposeQuest. Do something this month to increase your understanding of who you are, how you work best, and how your style interfaces with other styles for optimal team performance. It doesn't matter what profile you choose. It's only important that you take deliberate steps to grow in your understanding of you, and then encourage others you work with to do the same. If I can help you with this, please contact me.

If you have already taken a profile in the past, find the results and review them. I do this regularly and it is always helpful. In fact, every time I read my results report, I learn something new, so I am speaking from personal experience. Learn more about who *you* are and who the others around you are as well. (I also had my team's profiles before me whenever I did evaluations or had to address some issue or challenge in their work.)

Purpose in the Family

We have discussed the role parents play in their children becoming men and women of purpose. I want to focus on three parents in the Old Testament, make some comments on how effective they were as PurposeParents, and then actually give them a grade. See if you agree with my rankings.

Abraham – Abraham was distracted at times by his attachment to Ishmael, whom he fathered with Hagar while he was waiting for God's promised son. To his credit, Abraham got involved in finding Isaac a wife, but Isaac wasn't what I would call a purpose-driven man. On the other hand, Abraham was willing to sacrifice his son at God's command, which shows he certainly put God before his son and had his priorities in the right order.

What did Isaac ever accomplish? Not much. We will see that Isaac was a poor father. Therefore, I conclude that Abraham failed to provide adequate direction for Isaac, whose only accomplishment seems to have been re-opening some of his father's wells the locals had filled in.

Isaac obviously knew about the promises God made to Abraham, but did little to carry them out. For that, I give Abraham a C as a PurposeParent.

Isaac – As you can tell, I am not a big fan of Isaac. Rebekah had to intervene in the family's affairs quite often and Isaac didn't seem to pay attention. No one will ever convince me Isaac didn't know it was Jacob standing before him when Jacob tricked Isaac into giving him the blessing belonging to the eldest: "Jacob went close to his father Isaac, who touched him and said, 'The voice is the voice of Jacob, but the hands are the hands of Esau.' He did not recognize him, for his hands were hairy like those of his brother Esau; so he blessed him. 'Are you really my son Esau?' he asked" (Genesis 27:22-24). Isaac did not want to confront Jacob or make his wife angry, so he went along with the ploy (author's opinion).

Isaac was seldom (if ever) mentioned by Jacob, and because of Isaac's poor parenting model, Jacob's family was a mess. I give Isaac an F as a PurposeParent.

Jacob – What can we say about a man who played favorites, didn't confront the obvious animosity between his sons, fathered sons to four different women, and paid more attention to his business than to his offspring? We would say that he was a bad parent, and that's what Jacob was. I give Jacob a D as a parent (at least he had the sense to favor Joseph over the rest, although the way he did it caused Joseph tremendous problems).

At this point, I want to go one step further. I would give Jacob an A as a grandfather. Read Genesis 48:1-22 and see how Jacob handled blessing Joseph's sons. He got it right. He didn't pay attention to age, but to ability and God's blessing. He refused to cooperate with what Joseph wanted him to do and instead released and endorsed each grandchild to his divine destiny.

PurposeCoach Tips

As a parent, meditate on and discuss with other parents the parenting skills of Abraham, Isaac, and Jacob as they relate to your child's purpose. What can you learn about what *not* to do with your children? What can you learn that will make you more effective? Can you think of other parental models to consider from the Bible? How about Mary, Moses' parents, Hannah, Jesse, or David? What can you learn from them that will cause your children to be more in tune with their purpose and destiny?

Personal Purpose

Finding personal purpose can be hard work. To corroborate this truth, I again quote from Laurence Boldt's book, *How to Find the Work You Love*:

The quest for the work you love—it all begins with the two simple questions: Who am I? And What in the world am I doing here? While as old as humanity itself, these perennial questions are born anew in every man and woman who is privileged to walk upon this earth. Every sane man and woman, at some point in his or her life, is confronted by these questions—some while but children; more in adolescence and youth; still more at midlife or when facing retirement; and even the toughest customers at the death of a loved one or when they themselves have a brush with death. Yes, somewhere, sometime, we all find ourselves face to face with the questions, Who am I? and What am I here for?

And we do make some attempt to answer them. We ask our parents and teachers, and it seems they do not know. They refer us to political and religious institutions, which often crank out canned answers devoid of personal meaning. Some even tell us that life has no meaning, save for eating and breeding. Most of us are smart enough to recognize that canned answers or begging the question will not do. We must find real answers for ourselves. But that takes more heart and effort than we are often willing to give.

Finding the work you love is not a cerebral process. It is not a matter of figuring something out through a process of rational analysis. It is a process of opening yourself and beginning to pay attention to what you respond to with energy and enthusiasm. Pay attention to the people, events, and activities in the outside world that evoke the strongest response from you. Pay attention as well to your inside world, to the inspirations and intuitions that most excite you. From within and without, let yourself be moved. Listen to your own heart and learn to trust what it is saying.[13]

What word of wisdom can I give you concerning personal purpose? It would be the last line from the above quote: "Listen to your own heart and learn to trust what it is saying." You as a believer should have the inside track to do just that. Go to www.purposequest. com, download some of the articles, read some past *Monday Memos* at www.stankomondaymemo.com, and then listen to what your heart is telling you. Also, find a mentor or coach who can help you sort out what you're hearing. If you do all that, you will be well on the way to clarifying your life's purpose.

CHAPTER 7

Purpose Brings Pain

A man named Saul, who later became known as Paul the Apostle, encountered his purpose one day on a road leading to Damascus. He called it a light from heaven. Purpose doesn't come from personal enlightenment or from self-discovery. Purpose is a revelation. Consider Saul's experience:

> On one of these journeys I was going to Damascus with the authority and commission of the chief priests. About noon, O king, as I was on the road, *I saw a light from heaven, brighter than the sun, blazing around me and my companions.* We all fell to the ground, and I heard a voice saying to me in Aramaic, . . . So then, King Agrippa, *I was not disobedient to the vision from heaven"* (Acts 26:12–14, 19, emphasis added).

Saul walked away from that road and went down another road, the road called purpose. That road brought him much success and fulfillment, but also brought him a lot of hard work and pain. He saw what he called a light from heaven and cooperated with the purpose God had for him. He lived another 30 years after his encounter with God on the Damascus road, planted churches, wrote letters or epistles to those churches, and was martyred for his faith in the God of his purpose. He still speaks out of the power of his purpose to those who will listen:

> I have worked much harder, been in prison more frequently, been flogged more severely, and been exposed to death again and again. Five times, I received from the Jews the forty lashes minus one. Three times I was beaten with rods, once I was stoned, three times I was shipwrecked, I spent a night and a day in the open sea, I have been constantly on the move, I have been in danger from rivers, in danger from bandits, in danger from my own countrymen, in danger from Gentiles; in danger in the city, in danger in the country, in danger at sea; and in danger from false brothers. I have labored and toiled and have often gone without sleep; I have known hunger and thirst and have often gone without food; I have been cold and naked. Besides everything else, I face daily the pressure of my concern for all the churches. Who is weak, and I do not feel weak? (2 Corinthians 11:23-29).

Saul is arguably an extreme case. The nature of his pioneering work led him to face much more than most of us will ever encounter, but the principle still holds true: Your purpose will lead you to some painful experiences. In fact, that can be another indicator of what your purpose truly is.

Over what do you weep? What consistently angers you? If wasted resources angers you, maybe you are to conserve and preserve? If inefficiency frustrates you, maybe you are to be a model of efficiency, finding better ways to do old or new things? If seeing people not being used properly at work or in the church causes you pain, maybe your purpose is to find ways to best utilize human resources?

While purpose exhilarates and allows you to "feel God's pleasure," it also opens up a world of need that can be overwhelming. You feel the pain of others and sometimes of God due to a broken and fallen world. Your purpose gives you a heightened awareness to certain problems and you can't get away from the burden to get involved. Remember, God so loved people that He sent someone (paraphrase of John 3:16). God wants to send you into a world that desperately needs you and what you have to offer.

The pain keeps some from seeking or finding purpose. They know the cost that awaits them and intuitively seek safer ground in busy work, family, or church life. It can be a difficult job identifying their purpose, but more difficult carrying it out. That can keep them from seriously searching and being content with a vague definition.

Years ago, I was complaining to the Lord that I was too busy and under too much pressure. I began a two-week "search" to identify areas I could eliminate from my schedule and world. Then one morning, I awoke with a verse on my mind. I went to my Bible and this is what I read: "But by the grace of God I am what I am, but his grace to me was not without effect. No, I worked harder than all of them—yet not I, but the grace of God that was with me" (1 Corinthians 15:10). My search ended with the realization that my purpose— order out of chaos—was going to require not just what I was giving, but more if I was to fulfill it adequately.

I saw then that hard work "came with the territory." Unfortunately, not all my hard work has been rewarded with the order I was trying to create. My own mistakes, the fears of those in charge, people who preferred the status quo, and some measure of spiritual opposition have led me to discouragement, depression, financially lean times, and even unemployment. I have stayed up nights, traveled 3.5 million miles as I update this book, and have prayed long and hard for answers and insight, some of which has not yet arrived.

When talking with others who have found their purpose, I have learned their stories are the same: exhilaration in finding purpose, but occasional pain in expressing it. Yet there is no other road to travel, no other lifestyle to embrace. For purpose is our due north compass point, keeping us on target and effective. I refuse to stop creating order because it may lead to some tough times or even failure.

Then there's also the pain of perfection. I know I am and will continue to be human, and part of the human experience is learning from mistakes through trial-and-error. I am reminded of the words of Henry Wordsworth Longfellow:

> The heights by great men reached and kept
> were not attained by sudden flight.
> But they, while their companions slept,
> were toiling upward in the night.

How about you? Will you stay in your comfort zone because you're afraid of the pain if you venture out? How long will you settle for being cooped up in a lifestyle that has no purpose or fulfillment? Or will you venture out into a world or purpose that can bring discomfort but also joys unspeakable?

I made up my mind a long time ago not to settle for anything less. I have tasted the ecstasy of purpose and there is no turning back. There are many lives that attest to the truth of purpose, but can't seem to grasp hold of the specific reality for themselves. I want to speak to as many of those as I can before I depart this life. And I want to leave a written legacy that will speak to others after I'm gone.

There is one final pain point connected with purpose, and that is trying to find it. You may still say after reading these pages filled with quotes, coaching sessions, and stories, "I have no idea what my purpose is." To you I can only say, "Don't give up."

The poet, E.E. Cummings, once wrote, "It takes the courage to be nobody-but-yourself—in a world which is doing its best, night and day, to make you everybody else, [and that] means to fight the hardest battle which any human being can fight; and never stop fighting." It is a battle for some to discover the gold mine of purpose, for it is sometimes buried under generations of rubble, failure, and confusion—not to mention cultural pressure that demands you find a career and make money.

Your journey may include a string of jobs and experiences that have not defined what your purpose is, but what it is *not*. You may have eagerly set out on a course you were certain was the purpose course, only to backtrack to the beginning to start over again. Why this pain? Why do some have a Damascus-road experience like Saul, while others seem to labor in obscurity, answering questions for which no one seems to have the answers? The only answer can be in what I call the concept of enhanced appreciation. Let me explain.

When I go to a symphony orchestra concert, I enjoy the music, but I will never enjoy it like someone who has studied music all his or her life, who has spent countless hours practicing their craft or in rehearsals working out a good sound with dozens of others striving for the same thing. A person who has been through more than I to get to that concert has an enhanced appreciation of the final product, an appreciation into which I can never enter.

Your extra digging, searching, and false starts will only enhance your appreciation for the real thing. You will never settle for anything less once you've found the real thing. You won't waste a single minute on being anything you're not after you've spent your life finding out who are you. The pain to get to the destination will only make the arrival that much more special.

Before we move on, let's review. In these seven chapters, you have learned that

- Productivity is a priority.
- Productivity requires purpose.
- Purpose is personal and progressive.
- Purpose demand proof.
- Purpose is practical.
- Purpose brings pleasure.
- Purpose brings pain.

Armed with this knowledge, review and continue to work through the case studies and examples throughout this book. Check out the resources on my website. Read my books and the purpose books of others. Remember, "God makes everything for His own purpose, even the wicked for the day of evil" (Proverbs 16:4). With that in mind, don't settle for anything less than total life focus. If I can help you, don't hesitate to contact me.

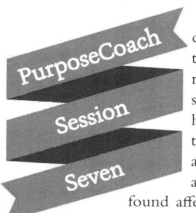

This is your final coaching session in this section, so it would be good to review what we have covered so far to see the progress you have made. In the next section, you will take a purpose assessment and then study a few more topics I have found affect your ability to find and fulfill purpose. For now, let's review what we have learned.

Purpose in the Church

I have described my experience in the church where we restrict the expression of purpose to those activities most common to church life: ushering, choir, children's care, and youth. We seldom make room for unique purpose expressions and we certainly don't look to fund any of them out of the church budget.

I outlined ways to incorporate purpose into church life in my book *Changing the Way We Do Church: 7 Steps to a Purposeful Reformation*, and I have touched on some of those steps in your PurposeCoach sessions. Those include:

1. Appointing a purpose pastor whose role is to promote purpose awareness in the church. Part of that role will require listening to what the Lord is saying to the people, reporting it to leadership, and then

strategizing to find ways to help people accomplish the assignments they receive from the Lord.

2. Hosting seminars and workshops to help people do what they are created to do. Those workshops would include how to start a business, how to begin a nonprofit organization, publishing, art, and missions.

There are more steps to take, but they require church leadership to change their thinking that the people exist to support and serve the church and understand that leadership exists to support and serve the people, as Paul stated in Ephesians 4:11–13 (emphasis added):

> So Christ himself gave the apostles, the prophets, the evangelists, the pastors and teachers, *to equip his people for works of service, so that the body of Christ may be built up* until we all reach unity in the faith and in the knowledge of the Son of God and become mature, attaining to the whole measure of the fullness of Christ.

CASE STUDY: Let's look at the life of a man named Joseph who you do not recognize or know by that name. Read Acts 4:36–37; 9:27; 11:22–30; 12:25; 13:1–3. Here are some questions to consider:

1. Why did the apostles change Joseph's name? Do you think Joseph was totally given over to his purpose?
2. Why did they send Barnabas on the described missions? Did it have anything to do with his purpose to encourage others?

3. How did Barnabas express his purpose? (giving, traveling, and preaching are a few examples)

4. How is this an example of the process I have described of the church using people according to their purpose and not forcing them to fit into the church's agenda?

5. Who was responsible for setting apart and sending Barnabas in Acts 13:1-2? Was there any hesitation on the church's part?

PurposeCoach Tips

Study the concept of servant leadership. While mostly found in secular literature, it is a concept consistent with biblical principles.

Servant leaders exist to meet the highest-priority needs of others.

You cannot take people where you have not gone yourself. Do what you do best and then help others do the same.

Purpose in the Marketplace

The concepts of servant leadership mentioned above have taken root in the business world, and the business section of a bookstore is where you will find most of the writing on that concept. I began studying servant leadership in 1998 and have read anything I can get my hands on about the topic since then. It has helped me realize that my power as a leader is to be given away.

As I give it away, I empower others but then a remarkable thing occurs: I find I don't have any less power, I have more, for I have multiplied my power by giving it away. Then God gives me more power in the form of confidence, knowledge, experience, and another leader whom I empowered becoming another servant leader.

The challenge for me was I had few servant leaders around me, so I had to pioneer the concept and then apply what I learned. That is why I have given away so much of my material through the Internet and social media. My goal is to influence others—the main activity of a servant leader—and that must occur without the power of my position hovering over the relationships with others. They must choose to do or be what I am proposing of their own free will.

PurposeCoach Tips

It is good business to place people in the right positions, which means a place where they have a chance to thrive because they are doing what they do best.

This requires that you get to know what it is that your teammates do best.

If no leader is present to help you, then you must do this for yourself, which may mean finding a mentor or coach outside of your business to help you develop and grow.

Purpose in the Family

Let's start this discussion with a case study, this time of a man named Samson. Read Hebrews 11:32 and Judges 13. What I want you to see is the role that Samson's parents played in his purpose. What lessons can you learn from this story to help you as a PurposeParent?

1. God may want to speak to you about your children before they are born.

2. God may be speaking to you and you aren't even aware it's the Lord.

3. Your child's purpose is important to God. He expects that you will help your child focus on their purpose. Proverbs 22:6 says, "Train a child in the way he should go, and when he is old he will not turn from it."

4. God wants to teach you how to raise your children to find and fulfill their purpose, not to find a paying job (Judges 13:8).

5. There is a rule for each child's life and work (Judges 13:12-13). You should seek the Lord for that rule or guide.

Can you see any other lessons here that will help you as parents to raise purposeful children?

PurposeCoach Tips

Try not to talk to your children about what they will do to make money when they are adults. Talk to them about what brings them joy and creatively search for ways they can follow their joy.

Let's look at three points that can help you and your children be people of purpose.

1. **A Nazirite could not drink wine or eat anything that came from the grape.** Wine is often a symbol of joy in the Bible. Thus, a Nazirite could not have any artificial source of joy for the duration of the vow. The Lord was to be his or her only focus and source of joy. Grapes have high sugar content, so even eating nutritious grapes was forbidden during the time of the vow. There was to be no artificial sugar "high" (and subsequent "low") for a Nazirite.

Help your children focus on what they do and enjoy and not on what they can do to make money. If they get joy from sport activities, encourage them in sports. If they love art, find a way for them to take lessons. If they are intellectual, promote and foster an environment conducive to study.

Help your child see that joy comes as a guide, not as a byproduct. God uses joy to direct His children into the activities He chooses for them. I have come to a simple conclusion that if you enjoy doing something, then you were created to perform that activity. If you enjoy playing the piano, then you should play.

If you enjoy watching sports, then you should watch. Remember the words of Nehemiah: "Nehemiah said, 'Go and enjoy choice food and sweet drinks, and send some to those who have nothing prepared. This day is sacred to our Lord. Do not grieve, for the joy of the Lord is your strength'" (Nehemiah 8:10).

If your child doesn't have God's joy (of if you don't, for that matter), they don't have God's strength. The only substitute for God's strength is our own, and that is always a poor substitute that leads to disappointing results. The Nazirite was forbidden to have any artificial source of joy; we aren't permitted to have any either.

2. **A Nazirite could not cut his or her hair for the duration of the vow.** In Western cultures, a lot of money is spent on hair products. People with curly hair want it straight; people with straight hair want it to be curly. People with brown hair want it blond and people with gray hair want it anything but gray. The counter culture of the young wants blue, green, or purple hair. Bald people want it to look like they have hair; people with a full head of hair often shave their head bald. You get the idea: We spend a lot of time thinking about our hair and how we would want it to be.

Hair is something we cannot control until it grows. It comes from below the skin. It symbolizes the inner life of each person that comes from God. God made each one unique as symbolized by that person's hair. We are not to try and change that person, but rather make that inner person the fullest, best expression of who it is God made us to be.

Often, we want to change things about who we are, but God isn't interested in us doing that—unless it is sinful or selfish behavior. At times, we may see someone we admire with gifts we covet, so we set out on a course to adjust who we are to be more like someone else. In other words, we fashion our spiritual hair into something that looks more like who we think we should be. The Nazirite wasn't permitted to do that. For the duration of the vow, the Nazirite had to let his or her hair grow; they could not touch the natural growth and development coming from within.

We need to help our children be content with who they are and who they are not. If they are introverted, don't push them to be an extrovert. If they love to organize, don't force them to build relationships. If they enjoy being with people, don't confine them to their room for a time of solitude. When you do those things, you are teaching them to put a razor to their hair—you are teaching them to tamper with the essential nature of who God created them to be. We need to help our young people not to compare themselves with others, but to celebrate who they are.

3. **A Nazirite was not permitted to have contact with a dead body.** While someone was under the Nazirite vow, they could not touch any dead body, even if a member of their immediate family died. The Nazirite was set apart for the duration of the vow (in Samson's case, it was for life), and

death was to have no place in their world. I wonder if this practice didn't represent something that Jesus tried to teach His disciples? "Anyone who loves his father or mother more than me is not worthy of me; anyone who loves his son or daughter more than me is not worthy of me" (Matthew 10:37-38). Anything that takes us away from life in God is negative, no matter how alive it appears to be.

We must teach our children (and learn ourselves) to avoid anyone who tries to talk us out of or discourage us from doing the will of God. We are to avoid any activity that doesn't produce or promote the life of God in our heart: "Therefore let us leave the elementary teachings about Christ and go on to maturity, not laying again the foundation of repentance from acts that lead to death" (Hebrews 6:1). And we are to abandon any thought or attitude not fostering the will of God in our lives. The Lord has one thing in mind for your children and you, and that one thing is life:

> This day I call heaven and earth as witnesses against you that I have set before you life and death, blessings and curses. Now choose life, so that you and your children may live and that you may love the Lord your God, listen to his voice, and hold fast to him. For the Lord is your life, and he will give you many years in the land he swore to give to your fathers, Abraham, Isaac and Jacob (Deuteronomy 30:19-20).

God is the only source of life for you and your children. You are to ruthlessly avoid or eliminate anything or anyone who may take away from that life, without exception.

Are there any other lessons from Samson's life for you and your family? I urge you to help your children think purpose and not occupations. Teach them to trust the Lord by trusting their joy, seeing iit as a compass that God uses to direct and guide his people.

There is no greater purpose legacy you can leave your children than to be a mom or dad (or aunt and uncle) of purpose yourself. Do you do what you love? Or do you come home every day from work moaning and complaining about the conditions or the work itself? What steps are you willing to take to connect with your joy? Don't just be content to talk about purpose; live it. Then your children will have a role model to follow as they too seek to be a Nazirite in the service of their purpose for the rest of their lives: "Train up a child in the way he should go [and in keeping with his individual gift or bent], and when he is old he will not depart from it" (Proverbs 22:6 AMP).

Personal Purpose

Let's continue our discussion of Samson that began in the family discussion. Samson was less than perfect, to say the least, yet he pleased God through his faith as a man of purpose. Read a little more of Samson's story found in Judges 13:24-16:31. (Even if you know his story, you may want to stop and read it again before you go on.) There are three points I would like to make concerning Samson's life of purpose and hopefully you can apply them to your own PurposeQuest.

1. **God is often leading you and you don't know it**. "Samson went down to Timnah and saw there a young Philistine woman. When he returned, he said to his father and mother, "I have seen a Philistine woman in Timnah; now get her for me as my wife." His father and mother replied, "Isn't there an acceptable woman among your relatives or among all our people? Must you go to the uncircumcised Philistines to get a wife?" But Samson said to his father, "Get her for me. She's the right one for me." (His parents did not know that this was from the Lord, who was seeking an occasion to confront the Philistines; for at that time they were ruling over Israel.) (Judges 14:1-4). Samson's family didn't understand what was going on and, for that matter, neither did Samson. God was leading Samson, positioning him to be right where God wanted him to be so he could do what the Lord wanted him to do. It may not seem like God is leading you, but He is. When you feel like God isn't there, that's not the time to trust less, but more. Put your hope in the God of your purpose and move on.

2. **Your past may hold a key to your quest**. "Samson went down to Timnah together with his father and mother. As they approached the vineyards of Timnah, suddenly a young lion

came roaring toward him. The Spirit of the Lord came upon him in power so that he tore the lion apart with his bare hands as he might have torn a young goat. But he told neither his father nor his mother what he had done. Then he went down and talked with the woman, and he liked her. Some time later, when he went back to marry her, he turned aside to look at the lion's carcass. In it was a swarm of bees and some honey, which he scooped out with his hands and ate as he went along. When he rejoined his parents, he gave them some, and they too ate it. But he did not tell them that he had taken the honey from the lion's carcass" (Judges 14:5-9). Samson did something he thought was gone and forgotten. Yet when he returned to it, even though it was "dead," it brought forth something sweet, which fed both him and his parents. What is in your past that you thought was dead? Is it a failure or something you enjoyed doing but don't do any longer? Perhaps it's time to revisit that and see if there is something sweet there? Often simple or overlooked things from your past provide keys to understand your present PurposeQuest.

3. **It's never too late**. "While they were in high spirits, they shouted, 'Bring out Samson to entertain us.' So they called Samson out of the prison, and he performed for them. When they stood him among the pillars, Samson said to the servant who held his hand, "Put me where I can

feel the pillars that support the temple, so that I may lean against them." Now the temple was crowded with men and women; all the rulers of the Philistines were there, and on the roof were about three thousand men and women watching Samson perform. Then Samson prayed to the Lord, "O Sovereign Lord, remember me. O God, please strengthen me just once more, and let me with one blow get revenge on the Philistines for my two eyes." Then Samson reached toward the two central pillars on which the temple stood. Bracing himself against them, his right hand on the one and his left hand on the other, Samson said, "Let me die with the Philistines!" Then he pushed with all his might, and down came the temple on the rulers and all the people in it. Thus he killed many more when he died than while he lived" (Judges 16:25–30). Samson was a miserable failure, or so it seemed. He was defeated, blinded, and forced to perform for his enemies. Yet he prayed and God heard him, and Samson literally brought the house down at his last performance. He fulfilled his purpose to the end, proving it's never too late to pursue or fulfill purpose.

So what about you? What lessons can you learn from Samson's life? How can you apply them to your current PurposeQuest? Is it time to trust God even though it seems like nothing is happening in your life? Is it time to reevaluate your past and see if there is anything there that can still yield something useful? Have you given up, feeling like it's too late to be a person of purpose?

If the answer is yes to any of these questions, then take out a piece of paper and start writing. Put down your thoughts as you study Samson's life, recording your thoughts and insights. Then use Samson's profile to encourage yourself in your own PurposeQuest. If Samson finished his quest for purpose it, so can you. Don't abandon the quest.

There you have it—the revised content for *I Wrote This Book on Purpose...So You Can Know Yours* and seven PurposeCoach sessions. How are you doing on your own PurposeQuest? Good? Not so good? To find out, I am including a bonus section that will begin and end with you taking a purpose assessment on my website. That will enable you to get some idea of where you are, where you need to improve, and then show if you are improving. Let's move on to the bonus section. (The promised items in the Appendix will be after the bonus section.)

BONUS SECTION
The Purpose Challenge

1. It Takes Heart

A few years ago, I developed a purpose assessment tool for the home page of my website. Since then, about 3,500 people have taken the assessment. The tool is comprised of 20 statements and those who take it respond to those statements making one of five choices. Then each person who finishes receives a score that indicates where I believe they are in their personal PurposeQuest. I thought it may be interesting to analyze the results as we begin this bonus section.

THE TALLIES, PLEASE.

When each person gets their score, I place them in five categories: Platinum, which is the highest, followed by Gold, Silver, Copper, and Bronze, which is the lowest (if I had it to do over again, I would not make the categories or feedback as complicated as they are, but it is still effective). Here is the percentage breakdown for those who got scores:

1. Platinum – 2%
2. Gold – 14%
3. Silver – 27%
4. Copper – 32%
5. Bronze – 23%

Eighty-five percent of those who have taken the assessment fell into the lowest three categories of the assessment. Along with each score, I also provide recommendations for what a person can do to move up to the next level of purpose awareness. I have no idea how many followed up with my recommendations, but I know a few enlisted me along the way as their purpose coach.

At one time, I analyzed three-month's worth of results and compared them to the previous 24 months and found that there was a five percentage points increase in the copper, silver, and gold levels, with little change in the highest category and a decrease in the lowest. It seems that people are increasing in their purpose awareness but it is a slow process. (I have not analyzed the last year, but it seems to me that scores continue to increase, which I would expect since there is so much material available now to help people understand purpose.)

What did all this tell me? The assessment and its results are hardly conclusive or scientific, but I do have some theories.

1. We are conditioned to think about jobs and career and purpose requires a radical change of thinking.

2. Purpose requires a change of thinking not only if we are going to find it, but also if we expect to fulfill it.

3. Discovering purpose requires time and effort, and we are already busy with the labor of career, family, and living.

This last point made me think again of a comment I read in Laurence Boldt's book, *How to Find the Work You Love,* quoted earlier:

> The quest for the work you love—it all begins with the two simple questions: Who am I? And What in the world am I doing here? While as old as humanity itself, these perennial questions are born anew in every man and woman who is privileged to walk upon this earth. Every sane man and woman, at some point in his or her life, is confronted by these questions—some while but children; more in adolescence and youth; still more at midlife or when facing retirement; and even the toughest customers at the death of a loved one or when they themselves have a brush with death. Yes, somewhere, sometime, we all find ourselves face to face with the questions, Who am I? and What am I here for?
>
> And we do make some attempt to answer

them. We ask our parents and teachers, and it seems they do not know. They refer us to political and religious institutions, which often crank out canned answers devoid of personal meaning. Some even tell us that life has no meaning, save for eating and breeding. Most of us are smart enough to recognize that canned answers or begging the question will not do. We must find real answers for ourselves. But that takes more heart and effort than we are often willing to give.[14]

Boldt says it takes heart to find your purpose, and I agree. Now, back to the assessment itself.

It may surprise you that not all of the 20 assessment statements relate to purpose. They also touch on the following areas:

- Goal-setting
- Time management
- Creativity
- Journaling
- Mentors and coaches

You may wonder why I include those concepts in an assessment of your PurposeQuest after all the material you just read in the first part of this book. Purpose does not stand alone as a pursuit in life. It exists alongside all the other skills and disciplines that will make you productive and effective. I will explain throughout the rest of this section why these concepts are important factors in your PurposeQuest.

For now, I want to issue a PurposeChallenge. Go to my website at www.purposequest.com and complete the assessment. You will automatically receive a score (and I will too). Then work your way through the rest of this section. When you are done, go back and take the assessment one more time. Let's see if paying attention to purpose and the other disciplines can blend together to make you more purposeful.

2. Have One or Die

Did you know if you don't have one of these you will most certainly die? No, it isn't one of your vital organs, but rather an activity or discipline. Well, it's really a mind thing or maybe even a heart thing, but if you don't have this thing, you will most certainly die. Having more than one will help you to truly live, and they will also stretch and cause you to grow. What is it that you must have? You know that to find out, you will have to read on.

A GOAL

If you don't have a goal, you will shrivel up and cease to exist in a short amount of time. Ah, but you may respond that you don't set goals and you are quite alive. Yet there is not an absence of goals in your life if you don't actively set goals. You are so built to set goals that you set them and don't even realize it.

You see, if you don't have a goal for tomorrow, then your goal will be to make tomorrow like today or like last Tuesday. If you don't have an income goal, then your goal is to have the same income you had last year.

If you don't have a ministry goal for next year, then your goal is to replicate the ministry you had this year, even if that was zero ministry. God created you to pursue goals so you will set them even if they are negative, neutral, or allowing for a slight change of what you previously had or did.

In the absence of a new goal, your goal for work is to follow the same path as always. Your goal for your relationships is to maintain those you have and not make any new ones. If your goal is not to make any new friends, you will achieve that goal. That's how powerful goals are.

ALONG COMES GOD

When the Lord comes into your life, He desires to breathe life into your goal-setting capabilities by freeing you from the hindrances that keep you focusing on the same goals day after day and year after year. Those things, like fear, small thinking, and unbelief limit you, just like they did the disciples who walked with Jesus. One day Jesus turned to his disciples after teaching a long crowd for many hours and said,

> As evening approached, the disciples came to him and said, "This is a remote place, and it's already getting late. Send the crowds away, so they can go to the villages and buy themselves some food." Jesus replied, "They do not need to go away. You give them something to eat." "We have here only five loaves of bread and two fish," they answered. "Bring them here to

me," he said. And he directed the people to sit down on the grass. Taking the five loaves and the two fish and looking up to heaven, he gave thanks and broke the loaves. Then he gave them to the disciples, and the disciples gave them to the people. They all ate and were satisfied, and the disciples picked up twelve basketfuls of broken pieces that were left over. The number of those who ate was about five thousand men, besides women and children (Matthew 14:15-21).

The disciples did not think they had enough to set a goal to feed the people. They did not focus on the possibilities or the power of God. They focused on what they had, or rather did *not* have, and they were ready to send the people home, just as they had always done. Jesus confronted their small and limited thinking and showed them what they could do partnering with Him.

What are your goals? Are they simply to keep your life the same? If they are, that is exactly what is happening. Are you ready to set some new goals, goals that will create a new tomorrow? If you are, then ask, "Where do you I want to be in this or that area of my life in the next year? What would I like to do? What do I feel God would want me to do?" When you answer those questions, then set some goals to go back to school, increase your income, write a book, or improve a relationship within your family.

Goals are essential to life. That is how God created you to function. You are already doing a good job, even if your goal is to achieve nothing. Now all you need to do is branch out and set some desirable end results and watch the same power that has been holding you back be used to launch you forward.

3. Role of a Goal

By now, I hope you have finished the purpose assessment on my website. You should have also received your purpose score, which also slotted you into an arbitrary category of silver to platinum (if not, check your spam folder). Now that you're done, let's set a goal for you to improve by 15 points when you take the assessment again at the end of this section. I found goal-setting to be one of the lowest scoring areas for those who have taken the assessment since its inception, so this will get you started on setting a new goal.

THE ROLE OF A GOAL

Why do you need to set goals? Why can't you just float along with the tide and go where the Spirit leads you? You can't do that because there are too many factors preventing things from happening in your life. You must play a role in the creation of the life you would like to lead. Paul outlined the dynamics of a goal in one verse, found in Philippians 3:14: "I press on toward the goal for the prize of the upward call of God in Christ Jesus" (NASB). Consider the words and phrases in that verse:

1. **I press on**. That means there is something pressing against you, and you must exert greater force than it is exerting on you if you are to make any progress. What are some of the things

pressing against you? Consider such things as laziness, fear, time and money constraints, confusion, and doubt, just to name a few. Feel free to add your own pressures to the list. Whatever you do, don't allow those forces to press and keep you where you are. Setting a goal will help you press through your opposition.

2. **For the prize.** A goal has a reward—achieving something you really want to do. Reaching the goal is the prize, and there is nothing wrong with competing against your own capabilities and the circumstances of your life to do something meaningful. A prize can also be lost or forfeited, so it is possible to set a goal and not achieve it. If you don't set the goal, however, you definitely won't achieve it. The prize is more special when the obstacles overcome were significant. Someone once wrote, *"There's no thrill in easy sailing when the skies are clear and blue, there's no joy in merely doing things which any one can do. But there is some satisfaction that is mighty sweet to take, when you reach a destination that you thought you'd never make."* The prize is reaching the destination you thought was impossible.

3. **Is upward.** A goal brings you closer to God and develops godliness in your character. The struggle and faith work something in you like nothing else can. You grow when you set a goal and make it, and the growth is almost as

good—if not better—than the achievement. My writing and speaking have blessed a lot of people, but I have gained much more than I've given. I've learned about God and myself in the process and now I'm better equipped to serve Him. Don't stand around with your feet on the ground. Soar to great heights in God by setting and achieving some goals.

4. **Involves a call**. A goal represents a desire of your heart, something God put there in the first place or that has developed in response to God's work in your life. When you acknowledge the desire is there, you honor Him by recognizing that God is the caller and you are the called—you are simply responding to His will and initiative. I have seen many people get hung up asking, "How do I know this is what God wants me to do?" And I always respond, "How do you know it *isn't*?" Then I quote Proverbs 16:3 from the Amplified Version: "Roll your works upon the Lord [commit and trust them wholly to Him; He will cause your thoughts to become agreeable to His will, and] so shall your plans be established and succeed." If your heart is to do God's will before you know what it is, God will direct your thoughts into His plan for you.

SO NOW WHAT?

We will continue our study of goals in the next chapter, examining the common enemies we have in the goal-setting and achieving process. For now, you can begin your emphasis on goals by identifying things you would like to accomplish in the areas of work, ministry, family, finances, and personal development. Identify any other categories and write down some ideas or things you would like to achieve. Don't get too formal yet; just jot down some ideas. Continue to study Philippians 3:14 to see if you get any more insight into the role of a goal. Don't be content to study a goal, however; don't stop until you set some. Better yet, don't stop until you *achieve* some. The endurance you learn will go a long way toward helping you persevere in your search for purpose.

4. Two in Three

In this chapter, let's identify and discuss your three enemies as you attempt to set and achieve your goals. This is important because they are the same enemies you face as you search for purpose. Which one of the following three is your most formidable opponent?

GOAL ENEMIES

1. **Unbelief.** It's an amazing process to see how quickly you can talk yourself out of a potential goal. Within five minutes of the initial thought, you can determine that you are too old, young, ignorant, poor, or unprepared to do whatever it is you were considering. And these thoughts

thwart your actions, thus cutting short the faith process. James wrote, "In the same way, faith by itself, if it is not accompanied by action, is dead" (James 2:17). For instance, let's say you want to write a book. Why don't you? You may not know who will publish the book so therefore you don't write. This is unbelief. Just because you don't know who will publish the book doesn't mean you shouldn't write it. In fact, no one can publish a book you don't write. Therefore, you do what you can do—write— and trust God to do what He can do—find a publisher.

2. **Fear of failure**. I have written a lot about fear and our ambivalence about failure. That is why I promote a regular "Celebrate a Failure Day" so that you and others like you can understand the role of failure in the productivity process. It works like this (we discussed this in the previous section, but it is worth repeating). Would you agree that failure can be a great teacher? Would you further agree that you can often learn more from failure than success? And would you also agree that you are always to grow and learn as you serve God and His world? If you answered "yes" to all these questions, then I have one more question. If those statements are true, then shouldn't you fail as often as possible? If you can see the truth behind that thought process, you will set

as many goals as possible, not worrying about whether or not you fail. No one ever kicked a goal or hit a home run that won a game if they were afraid to try. Yes, they may miss, but they also may achieve their goal because they tried. The same is true for you no matter what you are trying to do.

3. **Lack of diligence.** You may set a goal and establish a date when it is to be accomplished. What should you do if that date comes and goes and you haven't achieved your goal? You should determine if the goal represents something you still want to do and, if it is, set a new target date. Don't abandon the goal; extend the deadline. Goal-setting isn't a science; it's an art. You don't ever have perfect knowledge of the future when you set a goal. Often, you can underestimate what it will take to get the job done. When that happens, and it will, don't give up. Renew your efforts and keep trying. So what if it takes seven years instead of seven months? When you work on a goal, the goal also works on you. It helps you increase your faith as you pay a price to see the goal achieved. There is so much we don't understand when we set a goal, but the goal will keep us on course while we go through the unexpected detours we encounter on the road.

TWO IN THREE

Now that you have identified your enemy, it's time

to set some goals. I want you to look at three areas of your life—personal development, spiritual, and family—and set two goals for each area that you will achieve in the next six weeks. You can set a goal to read a book or books, register to take a class, read the New Testament, or visit some family twice in that time period. You may set a goal to have your purpose statement by then. I don't care what you set or how simple it is, just name it.

In the next chapter, we will look at ways to keep your goals in front of you. In the meantime, don't make this harder than it is. Remember, your assignment is to set six goals to be done in the next six weeks.

5. Get Over It

In this bonus section, I am writing about goals, mentors, time management, and other topics as a means to live a more purposeful life. We looked at goals in the previous two chapters. In the last chapter, I gave you an assignment to set two goals in each of three areas of your life. How did you do? In case you struggled with setting your goals, this chapter will explain why.

YOU CAN'T GIVE AWAY WHAT YOU DON'T HAVE

I have met with more than 3,000 people in the last twenty years to conduct what I call a PurposeProfile. It involves 90 minutes and a battery of simple personality assessments that help people understand who they are and how they function best. One of the profiles is a values profile and one of the values it measures is called "personal freedom." I would estimate that 90% of the people I assess have their lowest score in this value. What does that indicate? It's a strong indicator the people struggle with doing things for themselves, and that includes setting goals.

Some people are concerned they may behave selfishly, so they refuse to pay much attention to self-development. At the same time, they are eager to do God's will so they will do almost anything that comes along, whether it is suited to what they do best or not. While this is noble and commendable, it is not the best way to find and fulfill their purpose. What's more, they will never achieve excellence in any area of work or ministry if they don't pay the price to produce excellence in an area about which they are passionate.

When I attended my daughter's college graduation, the speaker asked each person present if they had a vision for their own life and future. Maybe you should ask yourself the same question: Do you have a vision for your life? Where will you be five or more years from now? What do you see yourself doing then?

The answers to those questions leads to another question: What are you doing about that today? What steps are you taking now to help you fulfill your personal vision? Are you taking courses on your own? Reading books on a certain topic? Considering a job change to enhance your professional development? What are you doing to fulfill the personal vision you have? If you are going to lay down your life for the Lord in His service, you must have a life to give away in the first place. You can't give away what you don't have.

SELF IS NOT ALWAYS SELFISH

What I just described may sound selfish to you. I'm not talking about a selfish pursuit that steps on others or serves self at all costs. What I am talking about is something you do that is in the best interests of the vision you have for yourself, the vision God gave you. If you are or want to be a doctor, then it's in your best self-interest to work at the best clinic or under superb mentors. Those things will help you be the best doctor you can be and serve your patients with distinction. If you have a desire to take piano lessons, find the best teacher around, regardless of their religious affiliation. If you want to be the best, you must work with the best. Too often I talk to people who are afraid of what others will think and therefore they play "small" as we used to say in basketball. If you're a giant but don't want to go near greatness for fear of what others think, that's not humility or nobility. That's just dumb.

I am reminded of the words of Frederick Buechner: "There are all different kinds of voices calling you to all different kinds of work, and the problem is to find out which is the voice of God rather than Society, say, or the Superego, or Self-Interest. The place God calls you to is the place where your deep gladness and the world's deep hunger meet."

I want to be the best consultant, writer, and speaker I can be. That is who I am, who God wants me to be. By investing to be the best, I am serving God and the world around me. I have a vision for what I want to do in five years and I am taking steps to fulfill that, by God's grace. What about you? If you think that is somehow ungodly or selfish, then I have a brief word of advice for you: Get over it.

Is there anything you can do that will bring you closer to your self-vision? What goals can you set? Maybe you can enroll in college and receive your diploma in the coming years. Why not apply this week? Perhaps you will open your business. Call someone who can help you do that, and take them to lunch. Or maybe now is the time to ask yourself, "Where do I want to be in five years?" Then allow yourself to formulate an answer.

Whatever you do, take a step that will bring you closer to your God-given destination. Don't consider this selfish and don't invest your preparation time in noble but frivolous activities. Focus on being the best, *then* feel free to give yourself away in the service of God and your purpose.

6. To or Through?

Recently, I visited Israel with a group of 36 others. As soon as I got home, what do you think I did? I set up my next tour to take place two years after this one. I did that because goal-setting is a way of life for me. Some of them I achieve, some of them I partially reach, and some don't seem to go anywhere at all. Yet I am never deterred or discouraged from setting goals. For example,

1. I spend so much time in Africa because I never leave Africa before I have my next trip planned.

2. Before I publish a book, I have a goal for the next book in mind.

3. I have goals for the next three months, the next year, and the next five years.

Why is this so important? It is important because productive people have learned to set goals *through* a point and not *to* a point. Let me explain.

TO OR THROUGH?

If your goal is to finish the work week and get to the weekend, you may not enjoy the weekend. Why? You set a goal to a point, which was Friday, but not through the Friday to what you will do once you reach the weekend. Consequently, you lose focus and energy, and end up wasting the weekend you wanted so desperately to reach. You can set a goal to finish college, but if you don't have a goal for after college, then you may have trouble finding a job.

You may be thinking, "How does he know if he can make his next trip or finish and publish his next book?" The answer is, I don't! If I don't set those goals, however, I may never achieve what is possible. I would rather fall short in the goal than to set no goals at all, and consequently fall short of my potential.

The process has worked by God's grace, since I have written 40 books, been to Africa countless times, and Israel on thirteen occasions. If you disagree with my process, let me know yours—but also let me know what you have accomplished with your process. If you haven't achieved as much as you would like to at this point in your life, then I suggest you overcome your reservations and employ what I am describing here.

Look at how Paul used this technique of setting goals through a point and not just to a point in Romans 15:24-28:

> I plan to do so when I go to Spain. I hope to see you while passing through and to have you assist me on my journey there, after I have enjoyed your company for a while. Now, however, I am on my way to Jerusalem in the service of the Lord's people there. For Macedonia and Achaia were pleased to make a contribution for the poor among the Lord's people in Jerusalem. They were pleased to do it, and indeed they owe it to them. For if the Gentiles have shared in the Jews' spiritual blessings, they owe it to the Jews to share with them their material blessings. So after I have completed this task and have made sure that they have received this contribution, I will go to Spain and visit you on the way.

Paul was setting a goal to visit Spain and he had not yet accomplished his goal of going to Jerusalem. He knew the power of this principle, so he was setting goals so his creative energy did not wane but would be sufficient to see him through to Spain.

What goals can you set even though you are still working on some older goals? Don't wait until you reach your goals to set new ones and, as you learn to apply this to every area of your life, your assessment score will certainly increase, which is just another way of saying that you will be a more productive and purposeful person.

7. A Values-Driven Life

I am regularly asked one question when I teach on goals or productivity: "There are so many things I *want* to do and feel like I *need* to do—how can I find the time to do them?" My answer is that you cannot find time; you already have all the time there is—24 hours every day. Often you must *stop* doing something before you can do the things you need or would like to do. I have found it important to clarify your values and then allow your goals and daily tasks to flow out of your values grid. Let me give you an example.

A SECOND DOCTORATE

One of my ten values is "I am a learner." I don't want to stop learning because then I will stop growing as a leader and person. Since learning is a value, I set a goal every year to read or listen to a book every month. Before I started my publishing company, I once read and listened to 55 books in one year. Do you see how that goal isn't something I *have* to do? It's something I *choose* to do. It is like brushing my teeth; I read every day because it is important to me. I don't even have to think about it.

When I was 61 years of age, I completed a grueling class schedule and study program to earn my second doctorate. I did that because learning is a value. What's more, I did it because I *loved* it. Identifying your values isn't the most exciting work you can do, but it's important work nonetheless. With that in mind, I have an assignment for you.

YOUR TURN

1. Go to my website and download the article entitled "How to Define Your Governing Values," an excerpt from my out-of-print book, *So Many Leaders, So Little Leadership*. Read through the article to learn how you go about recognizing and writing out your values. Don't worry if it seems a bit awkward. There is no wrong way to do it. You won't be tested; this is for your eyes only.

2. Set aside one or two hours soon. Get up early each morning, don't watch television this week, but do whatever you must to find two hours. Promise yourself you will do this and keep the commitment. (If you already have your values defined, it's time to review what you have.)

3. Once you have identified your values, you can then begin to set goals and daily activities focusing on things you value, things that should govern your life and time because of their prominent place in your heart and mind.

4. Most importantly, you may have a stop-to-do list that will free up some time currently devoted to the *urgent* that you can then invest in the *important*.

There is no shortcut to becoming self-disciplined and productive. If you are serious about answering the question, "How do I find time to do important things?", you must be serious about defining and writing out your values. This exercise is an important step in being more purposeful, so get to work and write out those values soon. Then let your values drive your decisions and guide your life of purpose and goals.

8. No Need to Pray

Did you do your work to identify and explain your values? If not, then I suggest you not move on until you have done so. Your values are an important part of your purpose progress. What role do your values play in your life? They help make decisions easier, for your values are so deeply ingrained in you that you don't even have to pray about your actions before you act in accordance with your values. Are you surprised that I wrote you don't need to pray? My purpose is not to shock you, but I stand by what I wrote. If you need further clarification on why I advise that, read on.

PAUL'S VALUES

Paul had certain behaviors directed by his personal values. We don't see that the Lord directed him to do these things, and his actions, while not unbiblical, were not directed by a clear biblical mandate. He didn't pray about doing these things; he just did them. What were some of his values?

1. He took no financial support from those among whom he worked (see Acts 20:33–35).

2. He built on no one else's foundation, but went to minister where no one had ever

been (see Romans 15:20).

3. He always went to the synagogue first in any area he visited (see Acts 13:13-15).

4. He traveled with a team (see Acts 16:6-13).

Paul's success in part was due to his development of and adherence to values that allowed him to do a great deal of work in a short amount of time.

DEEP-DOWN PRIORITIES

How do values develop in your life and work, and why are they so powerful to lead and guide you? Let's assume that at one time in your life you were homeless and penniless. This went on for some time and then God miraculously provided what you have today. If they approached you for help, you would do what you could to assist them. Your value would be so dominant that God would have to intervene to *keep* you from acting.

Another example would be if you have lost a child. You would do what you can to comfort and support others who also lose a child. Your value of compassion and empathy would move you to action. It's safe to say you would not even have to pray about what to do; your values would spur you to godly action.

Your values make your decisions to act easier and quicker. Your values also tell you where to devote your time and money, making your job of setting goals and managing your time that much easier. You must trust that God helped you establish those values through His work in your life, which is all the more reason you can trust them to help you make decisions pleasing to Him.

I gave you an assignment to write out your values. If you didn't do that, it's time to catch up. You can pray about your values but after that, the time for praying will be over and the time for action will be here.

9. What's in a Name?

If you remember, the purpose assessment you completed on my website is made up of 20 statements to which you mark an answer ranging from always to never. One of the statements I ask is this:

> 7. I listen well to others and remember their names easily.

What in the world does this question have to do with you being a person of purpose? To understand my rationale, read on to find out.

HARD TO HEAR AND REMEMBER

Have you ever been introduced to someone, only to forget their name as soon as you heard it? Isn't that embarrassing? It's often too awkward to ask the person to repeat his or her name, so you usually proceed to act like you remember when you don't. Why don't you re-member? You don't remember for a number of reasons:

1. It isn't important, so you don't invest any mental energy to remember.

2. You are nervous meeting new people, so the name goes in one ear and out the other.

3. You don't listen well, and so you don't even hear the name.

John W. Stanko

4. You are self-conscious, so you don't ask the person to repeat their name.
5. You don't repeat the name and use it in a sentence to help secure it in your own mind.

There may be other reasons, but those should do for this discussion.

THE SAME PROBLEM WITH PURPOSE

If you don't listen carefully, you may hear and not maintain your purpose or the clues that will help you understand it. People may pay you a compliment that holds a clue to your purpose, but you don't pay attention, so you miss it. Your mind may be so preoccupied that you hear but lose what you heard quickly. You may not journal, so you take mental notes, only to forget. The basic problem with hearing your purpose may be the same basic reason you don't hear names: You just don't pay attention. What is the solution?

The solution is to train yourself to pay attention and listen more carefully to what is being said around you? You can do this by:

1. Being more diligent to journal.
2. Ask more questions to ensure that you understand.
3. Share what you learn and hear quickly by teaching, talking to others, or writing.
4. Be more concerned with retaining what you hear than what others think about you.

Little things are significant where purpose is

184

concerned, and simply learning to retain another's name can be an important habit leading to other benefits. Start to pay more attention this week to others around you. While you learn a new name today, you may hear an important clue tomorrow that will unlock the secrets of purpose in your life.

10. Your Journal

In the last chapter, I wrote about listening to names as a means to help you pay attention to the subtle clues around you. They can help you understand your purpose. Now let's look at how you can maintain those subtle clues to build a purpose understanding for yourself or someone else.

WRITE IT DOWN

Let's first look at what the prophet Habakkuk said:

> I will stand at my watch and station myself on the ramparts; I will look to see what he will say to me, and what answer I am to give to this complaint.

> Then the Lord replied: "Write down the revelation and make it plain on tablets so that a herald may run with it. For the revelation awaits an appointed time; it speaks of the end and will not prove false. Though it linger, wait for it; it will certainly come and will not delay."

> "See, he is puffed up; his desires are not upright—but the righteous will live by his faith" (Habakkuk 2:1-4).

Habakkuk used questions to complain to the Lord and fully expected the Lord to respond. Therefore, he positioned himself to hear what the Lord had to say. That's faith. When he asked, He believed the Lord would respond. Are you listening when you ask? Do you truly believe the Lord can get a message through to you? How can you position yourself to hear?

Notice what the Lord told Habakkuk to do: Write down what the Lord was about to say. Why is that? The problem with taking mental notes is that the ink fades so quickly.

WHERE IS YOUR JOURNAL?

The Lord told Habakkuk to write down what He was about to say and to wait for its fulfillment. The Lord then uttered a verse made famous in the New Testament but which was an Old Testament truth: "The righteous will live by faith." In this context, the righteous will live by faith that God will respond. Part of the faith is to be expressed in writing and waiting. Most believers have the waiting down pat; few do the writing.

Your assignment is to secure a good journal (the nicer the better) and to begin regular entries into that journal. You will write what you hear in response to the questions you ask the Lord. You will also write about what you see, hear, taste, experience, and think about. No longer will you be uptight about what you write. You will no longer say you don't like or have time to journal. You will develop the habit of writing things down, just like Habakkuk did.

As I have studied the Assessment scores that have

come in over the years, journaling is a weak or nonexistent habit among those with lower scores. That is why we will write about this habit for the next few chapters. Right now, it's important you start or re-start to journal.

11. Christian-itis

In this chapter, I want to provide another reason why journaling is important: It helps fight the disease called Christian-itis. You have never heard of Christian-itis? It afflicts the mind and is able to shut down all your goal-setting and purpose-seeking efforts. It can even lead to paralysis of the will. Let's look at this debilitating but not deadly disease.

TWO SYMPTOMS

Christian-itis usually manifests in one of two ways. The first is an inability to think or talk about yourself, what you enjoy, or what you are good at doing. To do so is pride, or so Christian-itis tells you, so you avoid doing any deep searching or digging. Christian-itis tells you your feelings can lead you down the wrong path, so they aren't to be trusted either. Compliments cannot be received and processed, for what you do is only because of God's work in your life. Failures, on the other hand, are purely your fault and you must beat yourself up for any wrongs done and avoid again doing *anything* resembling the events that led to the failure.

The second way Christian-itis shows up is in extreme passivity. This symptom dictates that you must wait on the Lord for *all* things, careful to avoid any initiatives that come from your heart or emotions. If God wants you to do or be something, then it is up to Him to initiate, confirm, direct, guide, and finalize *everything*. You are the passenger along for the cruise and He is the captain, steward, purser, navigator, and entertainer. This symptom helps you avoid any success, along with any failure, and enables you to judge the efforts of others rather than engage in your own. You are able to blame the Lord for any inactivity on your part for you are waiting but He is not moving.

I am being facetious while exaggerating these symptoms—but not by much. Let's now look at how journaling can help you overcome Christian-itis.

PAY ATTENTION

Journaling helps you pay attention to what is going on around and in you. Why is that important? You want to write down what you think and feel so you can see it, honor it, and allow God to use it to direct you in the paths of righteousness. Faith without action is dead according to James in his epistle and journaling gives you a chance to do *something* with your dreams, thoughts, and faith ideas. Read what the Lord told the prophet who was complaining to the Lord about his circumstances (yes, it's the same passage as I quoted in the last chapter):

> I will stand at my watch and station myself on the ramparts; I will look to see what he will say to me, and what answer I am to give to this complaint.

> Then the Lord replied: "Write down the revelation and make it plain on tablets so that

a herald may run with it. For the revelation awaits an appointed time; it speaks of the end and will not prove false. Though it linger, wait for it; it will certainly come and will not delay. See, he is puffed up; his desires are not upright—but the righteous will live by his faith" (Habakkuk 2:1-4).

If the Lord directed the prophet to write it down, don't you think He may be giving you the same advice?

There is no wrong way to journal but to do it, but please don't use a yellow tablet or spiral notebook as a journal. Invest in something nice so you will be sure to use it. Get started and I will give you some more advice in the next chapter to help you navigate the PurposeChallenge. In the meantime, may the Lord provide the cure for any Christian-itis you may have.

12. A Poor Christian

It occurred to me that King David, before he was king, would have made a poor Christian. What would have made him one, you may ask? Something he did? Some egregious sin? Something he said? It is something he said, but it's not exactly what but *how* he said it that could disqualify him in many Christian circles today. If you want to know exactly what I mean, you will have to read on.

BRAGGADOCIO

Braggadocio sounds like an exotic vegetable in a salad, but it's not. It is an empty boasting or arrogant pretension, and that's exactly what it would seem like to some when we read what David said as he got ready to duel Goliath:

> David said to the Philistine, "You come against me with sword and spear and javelin, but I come against you in the name of the Lord Almighty, the God of the armies of Israel, whom you have defied. This day the Lord will deliver you into my hands, and I'll strike you down and cut off your head. This very day I will give the carcasses of the Philistine army to the birds and the wild animals, and the whole world will know that there is a God in Israel. All those gathered here will know that it is not by sword or spear that the Lord saves; for the battle is the Lord's, and he will give all of you into our hands" (1 Samuel 17:45-47).

Let's look at what David did *not* say in his response to Goliath's taunts:

1. "If it be God's will."
2. "Lord willing"
3. "If the Lord helps me."
4. "I'm seeking the Lord about doing something bad to you."
5. "I am asking God for wisdom in this matter."
6. "As soon as I have finished my college degree, I will kill you."
7. "Not me, but God's grace with me."
8. "I am praying about slaying you."

9. "I hope to slay you one day in the perfect timing of God."

10. "The Lord rebuke you."

David was specific and direct, and guaranteed victory in the name of the Lord. He predicted what he was going to do with confidence and clarity. Because he used the pronoun "I" and because he did not hedge his words, some would have heard David talk and concluded he was arrogant and boastful, or a poor Christian.

A GOOD CHRISTIAN

Is it wrong for someone to speak as David did, with such confidence and boldness? In a sense, David had a goal—Goliath's destruction—and he was specific and to the point. David promised God was going to help him bring down Goliath by cutting off his head and parading it around town.

Can you use a little more of David in your goal-setting? If who you are has not helped you obtain your goals to this point, may I suggest you need to change something, like your words, your confidence, and your faith? Goal setting is not what you *hope* to do; it is what you are *going* to do with God's help, but you must count on that help like you already have it. That is why David could talk about what he was about to do. David reached into the future and pulled it into today and thus did great things.

Your objective is to set some goals like David's. Stop fretting about whether they are exactly right or if God is with you. Assume He is, state your goals like they will be accomplished this week, and then take steps to make them happen. A good Christian is not one who talks nicely, but one who speaks his or her faith and then involves God in accomplishing the end result. It's time to slay some of your Goliaths and that may mean sounding less like you think a Christian should sound and more like David.

13. You Need Help

If you are seeking purpose, you need help, which may not be news to you. How can you get this help? In one of his epistles, John wrote,

> As for you, the anointing you received from him remains in you, and you do not need anyone to teach you. But as his anointing teaches you about all things and as that anointing is real, not counterfeit—just as it has taught you, remain in him (1 John 2:27).

You don't need anyone to help or teach you, according to John. Yet Paul wrote this: "It was he who gave some to be apostles, some to be prophets, some to be evangelists, and some to be pastors and teachers" (Ephesians 4:11). Paul declared teachers are one of the "big five."

John wrote we don't need a teacher; the other stated teachers are critical to our development as believers. Which one is correct? How can we resolve this contradiction? To find out, of course you must read on.

JOHN WAS RIGHT

John wrote his letter to believers who had teachers telling them that Jesus was not the Christ. John called those teachers liars, telling the reader that they knew better. Their internal "anointing" taught them and bore witness that Jesus was indeed who He said He was. There were some things, according to John, that believers knew just because the truth was in them. They had no need for anyone to confirm or teach them.

One of those things believers "know," in my experience, is the truth about their purpose. No one can give or assign you a purpose or goals. They are in you and, when you hear or see them, they ring true. This is part of the "anointing" that John referred to, for they are something personal and directly assigned by the Lord Himself.

Yet your purpose and goals increase your need for the church and the "big five," which includes pastors and teachers. You can't stand alone once you find what only you can find and know—your purposeful work.

PAUL WAS RIGHT TOO

As usual, there is no contradiction in the Bible on this point. There are some things you know, like your purpose, but there are other things you need to learn, like doctrine, right behavior, and values. Your purpose sets you apart, but your need for coaches, mentors, and teachers makes you part of a team, and that team is often found in the church. This doesn't mean your purpose isn't relevant in the world of business, medicine, or education. It simply means you won't be as effective as you could be if you don't embrace people in the church who are assigned to instruct and guide you in the ways of God.

I hope you aren't waiting around for someone to

tell you what your purpose is. That is something only you can discover and recognize when it comes. At the same time, if you know your purpose and have set some goals, I hope you are part of a team that can help equip and train you to be effective and relevant. Purpose is personal but your expression of it is communal, and that's where some miss it. No one can help you find your purpose but many can help you fulfill it.

I have written in the past about your need for a personal board of directors, people who are living or dead who can train and teach you. (We will talk more about that later.) Who is on your board of directors? Who inspires you to better performance? Who challenges you to grow and develop? Who helps clarify your values and then ensures you live them? This would be a good time to clarify your purpose and then recognize and formalize your team of teachers and mentors who give you energy and direction. Make a list of who they are, or make a list of who you would like them to be. Don't be confused, however, about their role. Only *you* can find your purpose but only *they* can help you make it all God wants it to be.

14. Your Personal Board

When I discovered I was called to ministry but not to be a Sunday morning pastor, I was liberated from my false expectation of who God created me to be. I connect my freedom to what Jesus said: "You will know the truth and the truth will set you free" (John 8:32). The truth has the same effect in your life. If you *know* you need to grow and improve, then you are free to draw from others who can do what you can't so you can hone your skills. If you are a writer, who is helping you to be a better writer? If you are a parent, who are you drawing from that can make you the best parent possible? If you are a pastor, who are your models and how can they help you be more like them? Let me make some suggestions of how to employ this principle of coaches and mentors in your life.

HOW TO PICK A BOARD

Don't get locked into bad thinking. You don't need a mentor or coach; you need *mentors* and *coaches*. I heard one man say that we need to hear from many preachers and speakers because "man's soul is too big to be fed by one person." The same is true for mentors. You need more than one. What's more, mentoring isn't a lifelong appointment. You will change mentors regularly as the needs of your purpose and creative expression change. But now you're probably asking, "Where can I find these mentors?" I'm glad you asked.

A person doesn't have to be alive and you don't even have to know them for them to serve as a mentor or coach. Here are some places you can seek people who will help you in your pursuit of purpose and excellence.

1. **People in the Bible**. Who are your favorite men or women in the Bible? Why are they your favorite? They're your favorite because they have something you need. Go back and study that person's life. Don't just read about the person, take

them apart, so to speak. For example, the apostle Paul is one of my favorites, so I've chosen him to be a mentor. I read books about him, meditate on what he did, and pray to the same God who helped Paul be a man of purpose who changed the world. I ask God to give me the Spirit of Paul. Now you see how the apostle Paul can be on my board of mentors.

2. **Historical figures**. Who do you admire from the past? In my case, I admire John and Charles Wesley. I've studied their lives and how they founded Methodism. I've visited their home and cathedral in London. I've also worked with Methodists to see how the Wesleys' work continues today, 200 years after they have died. The Wesleys are on my board of mentors.

3. **Current leaders**. Who speaks into your life today? Please don't limit yourself to the church world as you consider this question and option. There are two men who speak to me. One is Seth Godin, a man who writes about marketing and using the Internet effectively. I read Godin's daily blog and have every book he has written. The other is Robert Greenleaf, the originator of the servant-leadership message. Greenleaf died in 1991, but I financially support his foundation and read

everything his foundation produces on servant leadership. Godin and Greenleaf are on my board of mentors.

4. **Peers and associates**. Whose input do you value among your associates and relationships? I have several people I meet with regularly who help me with my business and ministry. When I say we meet regularly, it may be once a year. We may email from time to time, but I regularly draw on their expertise in the area of editing, finance, writing, marketing, and business development.

IT'S TIME TO CHOOSE

There you have my board of mentors and coaches. It is also possible for experiences or places to mentor and coach you as well. For example, I go to Disney World regularly. The environment there challenges me as I study what they do and how they do it. I have one or two conferences I go to annually, and those conferences inspire and equip me. I also attend live sporting events and theater to see how they move and manage crowds, how they advertise, and how the players and actors perform at optimal levels under pressure. What do you do or where do you go that is a source of growth and inspiration for you?

Are you ready to identify your board of mentors? Use the categories I have listed and build a team to help you be more creative and pursue excellence. Write down who is on your team and formally ask any of those close to you to serve in this advisory capacity. Then begin soliciting feedback or evaluate yourself in key areas. Guard against the trap that you have "arrived" and that there's no time or need for improvement. Make sure you subscribe to the words of the psalmist in Psalm 141:5, "Let a righteous man strike me—it is a kindness; let him rebuke me—it is oil on my head. My head will not refuse it." Pray about who will have the honor of mentoring you and start drawing on their strengths so you can pursue excellence. These men and women will also serve to make you more purposeful, and that is the ultimate goal as we work through this bonus section.

15. No Such Thing as Time Management

In reviewing the assessment scores I have received, many people give statement 11 a low score. Statement 11 reads, "I am in control of my time." Some who gave themselves a high score on statement 11 then had a low score on number 17, "I approach every work day with a written, prioritized plan." Both 11 and 17 speak to your ability to plan your work and work your plan, a key component of purposeful people.

Time management is one of the toughest disciplines in life, but critical to achieving purpose and goals, so I thought I would devote the next few chapters to that topic. If you don't need any input on time management, then you can skip these chapters, but should spend the time you save reading up on how to tell the truth. Truth is, we *all* need help where time management is concerned.

A MISNOMER

Time management is the wrong definition of or label for what you need. You don't need help managing time, for time cannot be managed. It goes by at the same pace it always has. You cannot save it, slow it down, speed it up, or recover it once it's gone. You cannot manage time; you can only manage the events that occur within the time you have. Rather than call it time management, we should really think of it as event management.

Let me give you an example. There is nothing special about 6 AM, until you set your alarm for 6 AM. The wake-up call is the event that takes place at 6 AM so you can be at work by 7:30. That requires you to manage a series of events to ensure you are there on time. Those events include showering, breakfast, devotions, getting the children off, and the commute to work. There is nothing you can do about the 90 minutes to get to work from the time you get out of bed; those minutes will pass as every 90-minute segment of time has ever passed. There are a lot of things you can do, however, to manage the *events* that occur in those 90 minutes. What you do in that period will determine whether or not you are successful, defined as being on time or late for work.

The rest of your life is like that as well. You have 24 hours every day; you just don't know how many 24-hour units you have ahead of you. My mother passed away at 92 years of age; a young child of five who attended my church was killed in a house fire a few years ago. Your times are truly in His hands, and you have the duty and joy of making the most of every day you have on earth.

You will do that by managing the events therein as best you can.

EVENT MANAGEMENT

You have all the time in the world. You have 24 hours for every day you are alive, the same as everyone else. Then why can some produce so much and others seem to struggle just to get through the day? It's because the productive person understands the difference between time management and event control.

Perhaps you should conduct a simple time inventory to determine exactly what events are filling the time you have. It's not complicated to do and you can read two articles I have about it on my website under the Archives/Miscellaneous/Organization section. You can get started today to identify where you are investing and spending your time. After that, you can see what you need to *stop* doing so you can embrace new activities and goals that will bring more joy and fulfillment, and are more in line with your governing values.

16. One Percent

As you look to apply the disciplines we have discussed so far, I ask you to commit to do something every day from this day forward. I want you to spend 15 minutes every day doing some planning for that day or week. I promise if you spend one percent of your day (those 15 minutes), then you can be sure the other 99% will be more productive than you ever thought possible. Along with the 15 minutes, here are a few other recommendations I would make.

A SYSTEM

Without a time-management system, you will find it difficult to keep straight in your head all that you decide to do. I used Franklin Covey (now I use my smart phone supplemented by my self-designed notebook portfolio), but I don't really care what you use. A yellow tablet is not a system, and neither is a spiral notebook or a bunch of small, sticky papers. You need a system to which you can add or take away, one that adapts to your world and needs. It must have room for notes, schedules, and any other recorded information you need.

You must carry your system with you at all times and agree to eliminate all "floating" pieces of paper you are always misplacing. I am in the habit of writing down all the things I would like to do so I never fret or spend time looking for where it is—it's in my system. When I sit down to plan, I then keep three things in mind.

THREE THINGS

First, I am proactive. I plan things every day that I want and choose to do, not those that I must do or are another's priority. That is how I have written my books and finished my verse-by-verse New Testament studies. I wrote them on my to-do list every day.

Second, I am holistic. I don't use my planner only for business or ministry. I use it for family, ministry, work, and personal projects. I am one person and have one day to invest, so I put everything into my system so I can judge all the activities by their comparative merits.

Finally, I am realistic. If I am busy with many things

on any given day, I don't try to plan too much, but I still use my system to make plans for some down time I may encounter. The beauty of a system is once I record it and don't get to it, it's in my system and I can reprioritize or schedule it for another day.

If you have a system, are you utilizing it to the max? If you don't, isn't it time you did? As you progress through this bonus section, I urge you to apply this chapter's advice immediately. Your time is the most valuable resource you have and if you use it properly, it will yield vast amounts of productive peace and harmony. Ignore my advice, and you will talk about what you want to do but seldom find a way to do it. Start investing your 1% every day and see if it doesn't add up to a bonus on the other 99%.

17. Your ABCs

In the last chapter, I urged you to find a time management system and learn to use it. Did you follow up on my suggestion? If you did, you are ready for the next step to help you increase your purpose assessment score. If not, you can still proceed with this simple process of ordering your day for maximum effectiveness. Ready or not, let's move on.

WRITE IT DOWN

I advise you to spend 15 minutes or 1% of your day planning the other 99%. I further advise that you be proactive, holistic, and realistic as you plan. Once you apply those principles, here is a simple procedure I have used for the last 35 years.

When you plan, write down everything you would like to do, need to do, or hope to do in the coming day or week. Don't evaluate what you think of yet, just write it down. In fact, get out your planner and do that for one day this week, preferably today or tomorrow.

Do you have your list? Good. The next step is to assign a letter value to each activity. The three letters you will use are A, B, and C. If the activity is critical and of highest value for the day, assign it an A on your list so that it looks like this: "A – Prayer, A – Bible Reading, A – Monthly report." Once you have identified all the As, then go through the list again and tag some of the remaining activities with the letter B, which are important things, but don't quite have the urgency of you're A activities. Anything that is left after A and B gets a C.

You are making a simple and quick clarification that all the things you thought of doing are not of equal value. You are making an attempt to sort them out by importance.

ONE MORE THING

Once you have the events on your list evaluated, now it is time to prioritize. Go back to your As and give them a number to identify the order in which you will attempt to perform the events. Your list will now look like this: "A3 – Prayer, A1 – Monthly report, A2 – Bible reading." Once you have done this with your A activities, then do the same for your Bs and Cs.

Once you have your list prioritized, follow it as best you can. Start with your A1 activity and stay with it until you are finished or until you must move on to the next event (A2). If you run out of time or unexpected things happen, as they always do, then you may have to adjust your list as the day goes on. The good news is that once something is written down, it isn't going anywhere. If you can't finish something today as planned, move it to another day of the week and start over. While something may be a B2 on Tuesday, it may become an A2 on Friday. That is how event management goes.

This isn't rocket science. In fact, it isn't science at all. It's an art form, something you creatively do every day as you manage your time. It may be a bit cumbersome at first, but once you get used to it, you will be hooked for life. (Ask me how I know.)

Enjoy your new techniques and use them to become more purposeful and productive. Once you have mastered these simple steps, feel free to adapt them as you see fit. For now, however, discipline yourself to follow my plan and you will become more productive and peaceful almost overnight.

18. No More Excuses

A few years ago, I read an essay entitled *Into the Wonder* about C.S. Lewis, the great Christian author and apologist, and one of the great creative minds of the last century.

AN UNLIKELY CANDIDATE

The essay began by describing a trying time in Lewis' life when he was living with his brother and an elderly woman. The woman was bedridden and increasingly used Lewis as an extra maid to help meet her needs. Meanwhile his brother, who helped him with correspondence and filing, drank himself to insensibility and ended up in a hospital. The pressures of this situation, along with his workload at Oxford, drove Lewis to the point of collapse and he was eventually hospitalized for exhaustion.

Shortly thereafter, Lewis had a friend over to his home to read him a portion of a new children's book Lewis was writing. This book became *The Lion, the Witch and the Wardrobe*, the first volume of the *Chronicles of Narnia*, which to date has sold 85 million copies in 30 languages. What is so interesting about this scenario?

First, Lewis wrote perhaps his most famous work at an inopportune time in his life. I feel like I can't be more creative or productive until certain things change, until my life is free of worry, anxiety, or mental clutter. Lewis didn't wait for the best time. In fact, in a time of suffering and professional busy-ness, he began to write fiction for children, an unusual creative expression for a man known more for his theological rather than fantasy work.

Second, Lewis was not married and had no children. (He had two stepsons from his marriage to Joy Gresham and did maintain a relationship with the boys after his wife's death.) It is remarkable that Lewis could write so effectively for children when he had none of his own.

Finally, Lewis was a loner as a child. His childhood, while not sad or abusive, wasn't filled with the kind of childhood joys upon which he could draw to write his stories.

NO MORE EXCUSES

Lewis produced creative work despite his personal difficulties. You must learn to do the same. You can no longer *not* create or be purposeful because circumstances in your life aren't quite right. Neither can you dismiss your creative ideas that stem from your purpose because you don't see yourself as qualified or worthy. Lewis was neither a happy child nor natural father, yet he wrote children's books that changed the world. What could you do if you stopped hiding behind excuses and limitations and did it?

Lewis' hardships prepared him to create and be purposeful; his suffering somehow fueled his drive to write. If you can see your suffering as preparation and not hindrance, you will find new freedom to produce when it may not seem like a good time to do so. Please don't tell anyone you don't have the time to create. You have all the time in the world—24 hours every day. It's not that you don't have time; you aren't using it to purposefully create. Together let's do things that will change our generation (and future ones) just like C. S. Lewis did.

19. Count 'em Up

As we continue to look at time management, let's look at come concepts from the word of God.

First, let's look at a verse from one of the psalms: "Teach us to number our days, that we may gain a heart of wisdom" (Psalm 90:12). I reflected on this verse and decided to do what the psalmist said: Number my days. Here is what I discovered.

As I write, I am 68, and that means I have lived a little more than 24,820 days. My father died when he was 79, so if I live to be my father's age, I have another 4,015 days. My mother passed away at 92 and if I live that long, I had another 8,640 days. That is how I numbered my days.

Of course, the truth is that I could have one more day or live to be as old or even older than my mother. That is in the Lord's hands. My job is to maximize the days I have left. I am determined to make the most of them all, wasting not one of them. Even if I have 8,000 remaining, that is still only a third as many as I have lived already. The clock is ticking and I am not sure when the alarm will sound.

WHAT ARE YOU WAITING FOR?

When you say you are going to do something "one day," something like going back to school, writing a book, going to Africa, or starting a business, when exactly will that one day be? What if the one day you assume you have is past the number of days you have left? That means you won't *ever* do what's in your heart, but will only have seen it from afar and talked about it. Why? Because you failed to do what the psalmist directed you to do: number your days so you can act with wisdom.

In a few chapters, you will have a chance to take your second purpose assessment as part of the PurposeChallenge. If you are going to improve your score, you must number your days—determining to make each one count by using your time wisely and with some sense of urgency. You can do that by having a plan for the coming days—a faith plan that will require God's help. Without it, I fear you won't number your days correctly and will lack wisdom.

I hope you have a ton of days left, but if this is the last year you have, how do you want to spend it? I have made my plans in the presence of the Lord, and I hope you have too. If you haven't, there is still time but it will start by doing the math and facing the fact that you won't live forever, so it's best to live today and tomorrow with zest and enthusiasm.

20. Two Secrets

One of the things we have been working on in this bonus section is how to act on the things in your heart with the time you have available. No longer can you put things off to another day. Instead, you think, "*This* is the day."

Some wait for more clarity and certainty before they act. Have you ever said, "If only I knew that God wanted me to do this or that," or "If only God would speak to me, then I would do it!"? While it sounds logical and spiritual, it isn't necessarily true, as we will see in this chapter. Who should I choose from the Bible to prove this point? If you guessed Gideon, you guessed correctly.

IT CAN'T BE ME

In Judges 6, we see that the angel of the Lord came to give Gideon his assignment of liberating the Jews from the Midianites. Gideon engaged the angel in conversation, explaining why he (Gideon) could not be the one. I'm sure you have never done this, but Gideon felt circumstances were too terrible and he was too insignificant to do what God was sending him to do.

Perhaps you have calmly explained to God and others the reasons why you are *not* the one to accomplish some great purpose. You have pointed out that you are too young, too old, the wrong gender, undereducated, or inexperienced. Even though you may have had an angel of the Lord visit you, you have dismissed the call as irrelevant, saying things like Gideon said: "'But Lord,' Gideon asked, 'how can I save Israel? My clan is the weakest in Manasseh, and I am the least in my family'" (Judges 6:15). It isn't always the case that if God were to speak to you, you would automatically do His will and purpose.

THE TWO SECRETS

God shared with Gideon two keys to success. Those keys worked for Gideon and they will work for you. The first secret is found in Judges 6:14: "Go in the strength you have and save Israel out of Midian's hand. Am I not sending you?" Gideon felt like he needed more strength if he was to go; the Lord told him to go in the strength he had and it would be enough.

You can put a whole slew of words in that verse and they would all be secrets of godly and purposeful success. "Go in the *time* you have; go in the *wisdom* you have; go in the *knowledge* you have; go with the *gifts* you have; go in the *faith* you have; go in the *money* you have." You won't get any more until you need it, so it's best to start right where you are today and obey God with what you have now.

The second secret is in verse 16: "The Lord

answered, 'I will be with you, and you will strike down all the Midianites together.'" When God speaks to you to do something, you become partners with God. You and God always comprise an insurmountable majority, no matter how improbable your success may seem to you at the start.

There you have it. It may *not* be enough for God to speak to you, for your bias against yourself and your abilities will try to overrule God. If you are going to go and do anything, you must go in the strength you have *today*, going with confidence that God goes with you. If you can somehow apply these two secrets to your life and purpose, you will stop wanting absolute clarity on what your purpose is and will go in the understanding you have today, trusting that God will give you more as you go—but not before.

21. What Are You Wearing Right Now?

One of the statements in the assessment you took is "I examine how I feel for clues to determine what I should or should not do with my life." Why is this a statement on the purpose assessment? It's difficult to walk in someone else's expectations, especially when those expectations don't relate to your purpose. You can try to please society, your family, and even your own understanding of what you *think* you should be or do, but eventually you will fail. It will deplete your energy and creativity and you will be miserable—and only you will know how miserable you are. So what's the answer?

It's simple; just don't do it.

You must resist every attempt by someone, well-meaning or otherwise, who tries to get you to fulfill their vision for your life. You must learn to have and pursue your own vision, for it is the only road to happiness and success. One of the directional road signs for that vision or purpose is the joy or lack of it in your own heart.

That's what David had to do before he was king and it served him well. You may want to read the story to which I am referring in 1 Samuel 17 before we proceed.

TRY THIS ON

The story of David and Goliath is known in many cultures and lands. Goliath and the armies of Israel lined up daily across from one another and nothing would happen—mostly due to Israel's fear. One day, David came to check up on his brothers and heard Goliath taunting the armies of Israel. That made him angry and he wondered why no one was doing anything about it.

When he heard there was a reward for the man who killed Goliath, David immediately volunteered to do the deed. When David told King Saul that he [David] would be the one to battle Goliath, Saul laughed, dismissing him as too young and inexperienced. David would not relent, however, so Saul eventually gave in and sanctioned the encounter. Before he let David go, he gave David his personal armor to wear:

> Then Saul dressed David in his own tunic.
> He put a coat of armor on him and a bronze
> helmet on his head. David fastened on his

sword over the tunic and tried walking around, because he was not used to them. "I cannot go in these," he said to Saul, "because I am not used to them." So he took them off. Then he took his staff in his hand, chose five smooth stones from the stream, put them in the pouch of his shepherd's bag and, with his sling in his hand, approached the Philistine (1 Samuel 17:38-40).

David could not function in Saul's armor because Saul was a head taller than all his peers (see 1 Samuel 9:2). Instead, David took off the armor and took up what he felt most comfortable with—a slingshot and some stones.

WHOSE ARMOR ARE YOU WEARING?

Do you see the lesson here? Saul had expectations that David could only fight dressed in body armor, so Saul gave him his. Others have tried to give you what fits them and you have tried to walk in it. It's not possible, however, for you to be a man or woman of purpose and walk in what someone else gives you. You must find your own joy, creativity, and passion.

What's more, you can't explain it to anyone because sometimes you don't even understand it. You know what your heart is telling you and that is what you must pursue, whether it makes perfect sense or not. Remember what the wisdom writer told us: "Each heart knows its own bitterness, and *no one else* can share its joy" (Proverbs 14:10, emphasis added).

You know how much you love music, art, travel, writing, business, preaching, or medicine. No one knows better than you what is in your heart, no matter how much they love you or well-intentioned they are. Only you are equipped to hear and follow your heart. Are you up to the task?

It's time to be honest. Are you trying to fulfill someone else's expectations for you? Have you put on someone else's armor? If so, take it off. Don't face your Goliaths in someone else's image of you. Face them in your own; that is good enough to get the job done. You will be lighter, nimbler, and happier than you have been in a while, and it will be a significant step toward identifying and embracing your purpose.

22. Talk the Walk

Have you ever said something about yourself or referred to something you wanted to do and then thought, "Why did I say that? What are people thinking of me right now? They must think I am boasting or have a big ego." If so, then that may be why you can't clarify your purpose: You are not comfortable talking about or drawing attention to yourself. Don't worry, however, for I have someone who can help you. Read on.

DID HE REALLY SAY THAT?

In the last chapter, we looked at one aspect of the story of David and Goliath. We saw that David could not wear Saul's armor when he faced Goliath. He had to wear and use what was most comfortable for him. I pointed out that you cannot walk in someone else's expectations for you, no matter how well-intentioned they may be.

David, armed with the right equipment (a sling and some stones), stepped onto the battlefield to face this fearsome giant. Immediately he was confronted with some daunting threats from this behemoth:

> He said to David, "Am I a dog, that you come at me with sticks?" And the Philistine cursed David by his gods. "Come here," he said, "and I'll give your flesh to the birds of the air and the beasts of the field!" (1 Samuel 17:43-44).

If David had been like some people I know, he would have said, "Well, maybe, I mean perhaps the Lord may want to use me, but don't get me wrong, I'm not saying I know for sure and if something good does happen, it will be the Lord and not me. I don't want you to ever think it's me." Fortunately, David was of a different mindset. When Goliath verbally attacked, David was quick to retaliate:

> "You come against me with sword and spear and javelin, but I come against you in the name of the Lord Almighty, the God of the armies of Israel, whom you have defied. This day the Lord will hand you over to me, and I'll strike you down and cut off your head. Today I will give the carcasses of the Philistine army to the birds of the air and the beasts of the earth, and the whole world will know that there is a God in Israel. All those gathered here will

know that it is not by sword or spear that the Lord saves; for the battle is the Lord's, and he will give all of you into our hands" (1 Samuel 17:45-47).

What confidence David had! There was nothing tentative in what he planned to do. He was bold and specific. Are you someone who considers talk like that offensive to God? If so, then you need to change the way you think. God isn't repelled by such talk; those words drew Him to David's cause, and He promptly went out with David to meet the giant. David made good on his promises, while Goliath died trying to figure out what went wrong.

TALK THE WALK

How can you apply this lesson to your life right now? First, David had a track record to which he could refer. He had killed lions and bears, and he saw killing this giant as a continuation of those exploits. You must allow God to put you in challenging situations so, when you overcome, you will be able to think back on those experiences to help you fight future battles.

Second, you must know who you are and what you want to do. David did not hold back; he was clear and concise. He said, "I am a champion of God and you, Goliath, are not. You are coming down, despite your size and confident words."

Finally, David said what he was going to do without fear of what others thought of him. He spoke positive, affirming, and powerful words and then set about to fulfill them, even though he was young—much younger than some of the soldiers, his brothers, and even King Saul.

What are you speaking these days? A better question is: What *aren't* you speaking? Tentative, faithless words produce tentative, faithless actions. Positive, powerful words produce similar actions. Stop being hesitant and fearful of making bold statements where your purpose and dreams are concerned. Dream great things, talk about them, and don't worry about how you sound to other people. Only be concerned with how you sound to God.

Many people are concerned with walking the talk, but if you aren't talking about what you are going to do with God's help, you won't have anything to walk. Dream great things, talk about doing them, and then go for it. It's simple to describe but not simple to do. I know that you can only do great things once you stop stumbling and mumbling through your purpose and dreams. You need to watch what you *don't* say and follow David's example of seeing and then speaking great things that will emerge as you fulfill your purpose.

23. What to Do with a Big Head

This is the last chapter before you retake your next purpose assessment and complete this PurposeChallenge. If you need to review before the big day, read some past chapters to help you improve your score. I have one more thought to share with you before we close this bonus section.

What do you do when you do something well? How do you handle it when someone compliments you for something they admire about you? If you're like some, you may not know what to do in those situations. You don't want to appear proud or egocentric, so you minimize your strengths and achievements in your eyes and in the eyes of others. This may seem spiritual or noble, but it's actually detrimental to the cause of purpose.

What should you do when you succeed or receive a compliment? For the answer, you will have to read on.

A BIG HEAD

We have looked at the story of David and Goliath in the last two chapters. Last chapter, we saw how David made specific declarations of what he was about to do to Goliath. David made good on his promises and killed Goliath with one stone from his slingshot. It's what he did next that answers the questions I raised: David cut off Goliath's head. That was one big head not only to cut off but also to carry around.

The armies of Israel were encouraged by David's win, and went forth to win a great victory over the Philistine army. That was one byproduct of David's success. Then David did something else that would be quite uncharacteristic for many people I know, perhaps even for you: "David took the Philistine's head and brought it to Jerusalem, and he put the Philistine's weapons in his own tent" (1 Samuel 17:54).

What did David do with the head? I doubt if he kept it in his tent or made a keychain out of it. He did what most champions did with such spoils of battle: David probably hung the head on a post for everyone to see. David celebrated his own victory and advertised his achievement. What's more, he kept a souvenir of the battle by keeping the giant's sword in his trophy case. How does that answer the question of what to do when you achieve success? Does this provide insight into how you should respond when you receive a compliment?

DON'T WORRY THAT A BIG HEAD
WILL GIVE YOU A BIG HEAD

David celebrated his victory. He wanted people to see Goliath's head so they would be encouraged to fight their own battles. As a good leader, David wanted the people to see that they didn't have to cower in fear. More importantly, David didn't minimize his success, saying, "Well, it was nothing. You know, it was a lucky shot and God really did it, it wasn't me."

Instead, David said, "Look what I've done. What can you do?" That's what you need to do as well. If someone pays you a compliment about something you've done or for something you are, say, "Thank you." Don't push their praise away.

If you have done something and no one compliments you, then compliment yourself. Admire what you've done. Savor the moment, without being self-conscious or worrying about what others may think of you. If you achieve a goal for which you have worked hard, throw yourself a party and invite your friends to celebrate with you. Take a trip in honor of your new job or degree, or for the completed project.

David knew how to celebrate his victories and use them to spur himself and others on to greater things. You need to do the same. Don't worry about a big head; there will be enough tough knocks and challenges to keep you in reality. When you do something great, don't be afraid to acknowledge that it was great. If others acknowledge that as well, then all the better.

This whole process can help you see that you should not be afraid of failure, but of what you will do when you succeed. Can you handle success and the admiration of others? I hope you will learn to broadcast your victories rather than hide behind mediocrity so no one is offended and you aren't uncomfortable. Aim for great things, do them, and tell the world if others don't do it for you.

24. It's Time

Now it's time to take your purpose assessment again to see how much progress you have made in this PurposeChallenge. As you re-take the assessment, give yourself the benefit of the doubt and not be too hard on yourself. Remember, this assessment is not sophisticated. It is simply a summary of things I have found to be important components in your PurposeQuest. Since measuring your progress of intangible things like purpose is a difficult task, you need to determine for yourself how satisfied you are with your current state of affairs.

Did you improve by at least 15 points? If so, congratulations. If not, don't be discouraged. Look back over the statements again and review the chapters in this Bonus Section that pertain to your weak areas. Then take the assessment again when you are ready. It's free and there is no limit to your number of tries.

Now you can browse through the Appendix to see if there are any other resources or thoughts there to help you discover your purpose. Remember, *I Wrote This Book on Purpose . . . So You Can Know Yours.* If I can help you as your PurposeCoach, don't hesitate to write or call. I look forward to hearing and adding your story to the many I have already collected, for I am confident if you do the things I outlined in this book, you will indeed *Know Yours.* Thanks for getting this far, and may the Lord bless your PurposeQuest.

APPENDIX I
Vocation and Calling

Some helpful quotes and thoughts if this terminology and perspective is more in line with how you think about purpose.

> Where your talents and the needs of the world cross, there lies your *vocation*. – Aristotle

> A man knows he has found his *vocation* when he stops thinking about how to live and begins to live. – Thomas Merton

> Within a few months of this time of consecration [his conversion to Christianity] the impression was wrought into my soul that it was in China the Lord wanted me. It seemed to me highly probably that *the work to which I was then called* might cost my life.
> – J. Hudson Taylor, missionary to China

There are three words that tend to be used

interchangeably–and shouldn't be. They are *"vocation,"* *"career,"* and *"job."* *Vocation* is the most profound of the three, and it has to do with your calling. It's what you're doing in life that makes a difference for you, that builds meaning for you, that you can look back on in your later years to see the impact you've made on the world. A calling is something you have to listen for. You don't hear it once and then immediately recognize it. You've got to attune yourself to the message.

Career is the term you hear most often today. A career is a line of work. You can say that your career is to be a lawyer or a securities analyst—but usually it's not the same as your calling. You can have different careers at different points in your life.

A *job* is the most specific and immediate of the three terms. It has to do with who's employing you at the moment and what your job description is for the next 6 months or so.

– Timothy Butler, director for MBA career development programs at Harvard University Business School

If you look at the derivations of the words *"career"* and *"vocation,"* you immediately get a feel for the difference between them. *Vocation* comes from the Latin "vocare," which means "to call." It suggests that you are listening for something that calls out to you, something that comes to you and is particular to you. "Career" comes originally from the Latin word for cart and later from the Middle French word for race track.

In other words, you go around and around really fast for a long-time—but you never get there. – **James Waldroop, director of MBA career development programs at Harvard University Business School**

Can you distinguish between your calling or purpose and your career? My calling or purpose is to create order out of chaos. I have never looked for a job, but each job that has come to me has allowed me to be true to my purpose. How about you? What calls out to you, like chaos calls out to me? Fill in the blanks below or use your journal for longer responses.

My calling or vocation is _____

_____

_____.

My career is _____

_____

_____.

Right now, my job is _____

_____

_____.

Your job and career can and probably will change over time. Your purpose never will.
– John Stanko

Blessed is the man who has found his work. Let him ask no other blessing. – Thomas Carlyle

APPENDIX II
A Closer Look at What We Know About the Apostle Paul, a Man of Purpose

1. Paul made tents for a living, but he never saw himself as a "tent maker." What did he have to say about his purpose? In every epistle he wrote, he referred to what he had been born to do and *never* did he write that it was to make tents. He was clear enough to talk about his purpose every chance he had.

- Romans 1:5, 13, 16
- Romans 15:7-29
- 1 Corinthians 1:17,24
- 1 Corinthians 3:5-15
- 2 Corinthians 5:16-21

- 2 Corinthians 10:12-18
- Galatians 1:15-16
- Galatians 2:2, 7-9
- Ephesians 3:1-10, 7-12
- Philippians 1:12-18
- Colossians 1:27-29
- 1 Thessalonians 1:4-5
- 1 Thessalonians 2:16
- 2 Thessalonians 3:1-4
- 1 Timothy2:5-7
- 2 Timothy 4:17
- Titus 1:1-3

If you have some knowledge about the Bible, you'll say, "Hey, wait a minute! Paul wrote 13 epistles and there are only 12 listed above. I thought you said he referred to his purpose in all 13?" Well, I did write that, and it's true. While Paul did not specifically mention his purpose in his epistle to Philemon, he was writing about an escaped slave who had become a Christian. The whole letter addressed a problem that was unique to the Gentile world, which was Paul's sphere of ministry.

2. The book of Acts, which chronicles life and ministry in the early church, spends a great deal of time relating stories of Saul or Paul and his purpose.

- Acts 9:15
- Acts 13:1-4
- Acts 13:47
- Acts 14:27

- Acts 15:3,7
- Acts 21:11, 19–21
- Acts 20:24
- Acts 22:14–21
- Acts 26:16–19

3. On six separate occasions, Paul had a vision or supernatural visitation. It is of interest that on each occasion, the visitation was to reveal or encourage him in his purpose.

- Acts 9:1–9
- Acts 16:9–10
- Acts 18:9–11
- Acts 22:17
- Acts 23:11
- Acts 27:24

4. There was a seventh occasion Paul described in 2 Corinthians 12 when he was taken up into the third heaven.

APPENDIX III
Verses that Mention Purpose

1. Purpose

Exodus 9:16; Leviticus 7:24; 1 Chronicles 23:5; Job 36:5; Psalm 57:2; Psalm 138:8; Proverbs 19:21; Isaiah 10:7; Isaiah 46:10; Isaiah 46:11; Isaiah 48:14; Isaiah 49:4; Isaiah 55:11; Jeremiah 15:11; Jeremiah 51:11; Jeremiah 51:12; Luke 7:30; Acts 2:23; Acts 5:38; Acts 13:36; Romans 8:28; Romans 9:11; Romans 9:17; 1 Corinthians 3:8; 2 Corinthians 5:5; Galatians 3:19; Galatians 4:18; Ephesians 1:11; Ephesians 2:15; Ephesians 3:11; Ephesians 6:22; Philippians 2:2; Philippians 2:13; Colossians 2:2; Colossians 4:8; 2 Thessalonians 1:11; 1 Timothy 2:7; 2 Timothy 1:9; 2 Timothy 3:10; Hebrews

6:17; Revelation 17:13; Revelation 17:17

2. Purposes

Psalm 33:10; Psalm 33:11; Proverbs 20:5;
Jeremiah 23:20; Jeremiah 30:24; Jeremiah 32:19;
Jeremiah 51:29; Romans 9:21;

2 Timothy 2:20; 2 Timothy 2:21

3. Purposed

Isaiah 14:24; Isaiah 14:27; Jeremiah 49:20;
Jeremiah 50:45; Ephesians 1:9

Endnotes

1. Laurence G. Boldt, *How to Find the Work You Love* (New York: Penguin Group, 1996), pages 1-2.

2. *Ibid.*, page 93.

3. Charles Handy, *The Age of Unreason* (Cambridge: Harvard University Press, 1991), page 180.

4. Boldt, page 20.

5. Richard Nelson Bolles, *The 1997 What Color is Your Parachute?* (Berkeley, CA: Ten Speed Press, 1997), page 226.

6. *Ibid.*, pages 228-229.

7. Curtis Coffman and Marcus Buckingham, *First, Break All the Rules* (New York: Pocket Books, 2006), page 57.

8. *Ibid.*, page 57.

9. *Ibid.*, page 91.

10. John Piper, *Desiring God: Meditations of a Christian Hedonist* (Sisters, OR: Multnomah Publishers, revised and expanded 2011), page 28.

11. Boldt, pages 133–134.

12. Marcus Buckingham, *The One Thing You Need to Know* (New York: Free Press, 2005), excerpt.

13. Boldt, pages 3–4.

14. Boldt, pages 1–2.

About the Author

John Stanko was born in Pittsburgh, Pennsylvania. After graduating from St. Basil's Prep School in Stamford, Connecticut, he attended Duquesne University where he received his bachelor's and master's degrees in economics in 1972 and 1974 respectively.

Since then, John has served as an administrator, teacher, consultant, author, and pastor in his profession-al career. He holds a second master's degree in pastoral ministries, and earned his doctorate in pastoral ministries from Liberty Theological Seminary in Houston, Texas in 1995. He recently completed a second doctor of ministry degree at Reformed Presbyterian Theological Seminary in Pittsburgh.

John has taught extensively on the topics of time management, life purpose and organization, and has conducted leadership and purpose training sessions throughout the United States and in 32 countries. He is also certified to administer the DISC and other related personality assessments as well as the Natural Church Development profile for churches. In 2006, he earned the privilege to facilitate for The Pacific Institute of Seattle, a leadership and personal development program, and for The Leadership Circle, a provider of cultural and executive 360-degree profiles. He has authored fifteen books and written for many publications around the world.

In 2001, John founded PurposeQuest, a personal

and leadership development company and today travels the world to speak, consult and inspire leaders and people everywhere. From 2001-2008, he spent six months a year in Africa and still enjoys visiting and working on that continent, while teaching for Geneva College's Masters of Organizational Leadership and the Center for Urban Biblical Ministry in his hometown of Pittsburgh, Pennsylvania. John has been married for 44 years to Kathryn Scimone Stanko, and they have two adult children. In 2009, John was appointed the administrative pastor for discipleship at Allegheny Center Alliance Church on the North Side of Pittsburgh where he served for five years. Most recently, John founded Urban Press, a publishing service designed to tell stories of the city, from the city, and to the city.

Keep in Touch
with John W. Stanko

www.purposequest.com
www.johnstanko.us

www.stankobiblestudy.com
www.stankomondaymemo.com

or via email at johnstanko@gmail.com

John also does extensive relief and
community development work in Kenya.
You can see some of his projects at
www.purposequest.com/contributions

PurposeQuest International
PO Box 8882
Pittsburgh, PA 15221-0882

Additional Titles by John W. Stanko